THE ANABAPTIST
EVANGELICAL PUZZLE

Discovering How The Pieces Fit

EQUIP PRESS

Colorado Springs

The Anabaptist Evangelical Puzzle Discovering How The Pieces Fit
Copyright © 2019 and Darryl G. Klassen (D. Min)

All rights reserved. No part of this publication may be reproduced, distributed, or transmitted in any form or by any means, without prior written permission.

Scripture quotations marked (ESV) are taken from The ESV® Bible (The Holy Bible, English Standard Version®) copyright © 2001 by Crossway, a publishing minis-try of Good News Publishers. ESV® Text Edition: 2011. The ESV® text has been reproduced in cooperation with and by permission of Good News Publishers.
Unauthorized reproduction of this publication is prohibited. Used by permission.
All rights reserved.

Scripture quotations marked (KJV) are taken from the King James Bible. Accessed on Bible Gateway at www.BibleGateway.com.

Scripture quotations marked (NASB) are taken from the New American Standard Bible® (NASB), copyright © 1960, 1962, 1963, 1968, 1971, 1972, 1973, 1975, 1977, 1995 by The Lockman Foundation, www.Lockman.org. Used by permission.

Scripture quotations marked (NIV) are taken from the Holy Bible, New International Version. Copyright © 1973, 1978, 1984, 2011 by Biblica, Inc.® Used by permission. All rights reserved worldwide.

Scripture quotations marked (NKJV) are taken from the New King James Version®. Copyright © 1982 by Thomas Nelson, Inc. Used by permission. All rights reserved.

Scripture quotations marked (NLT) are taken from the Holy Bible, New Living Translation, copyright © 1996, 2004, 2015 by Tyndale House Foundation. Used by permission of Tyndale House Publishers, Inc., Carol Stream, Illinois 60188. All rights reserved.

Scripture quotations marked (NRSV) are taken from the New Revised Standard Version Bible, copyright © 1989 the Division of Christian Education of the National

Scripture quotations taken from the Amplified® Bible (AMP), Copyright © 2015 by The Lockman Foundation Used by permission. www.Lockman.org

First Edition: 2019
The Anabaptist Evangelical Puzzle / Darryl G. Klassen (D. Min)
Paperback ISBN: 978-1-951304-11-9
eBook ISBN: 978-1-951304-12-6

Dedication

To my wife, Sharon, who believes there is more in me than I can see and reminds me daily of my God-given potential.

To my daughter, Katy, and my son, Ethan, who encouraged me to write.

To Trudy who said I should write a book on this material.

To Junia because she was the first one to say she would read this book.

> Even in social life, you will never make a good impression on other people until you stop thinking about what sort of impression you are making. Even in literature and art, no man who bothers about originality will ever be original, whereas if you simply try to tell the truth (without caring two pence how often it has been told before), you will, nine times out of ten, become original without having noticed it. The principle runs through life from top to bottom. Give up yourself, and you will find your real self. Lose your life and you will save it...Nothing that you have not given away will be really yours.

– C. S. Lewis, *Mere Christianity*

Table of Contents

Introduction — 11
    I Am a Mennonite — 12
    I Am an Evangelical — 15
    The Purpose of This Book — 17

Chapter One: An Anabaptist Confession — 19
    The Anabaptist Vision Revisited — 24
    The Anabaptist Movement — 27
    Core Values of the Anabaptist Movement — 29
    An Honest Appraisal — 33
    Are You an Anabaptist? — 35

Chapter Two: Seeking Evangelical Fervor — 36
    What It Means to Be Evangelical — 37
    The Response of Fundamentalism to Religious Liberalism — 39
    The Rise of Popular Evangelicalism — 41
    Modern Evangelicalism's Appeal — 42
    An Appraisal of Modern Evangelicalism — 44
    The Danger of "Jesus and Me" — 50
    The Problem of the Christian Nation — 54
    Conclusion — 61

Chapter Three: How We Read the Bible — 63
    How Evangelicals Read the Bible — 64
    How Anabaptists Read the Bible — 67
    Anabaptists and Biblical Inerrancy — 71

Chapter Four: How We Understand the Atonement — 74
    What Anabaptists Believe About the Atonement — 75
    Christus Victor — 78
    The Rise of the Satisfaction Theory of Atonement — 79
    Does God's Anger Need to Be Satisfied? — 81

Chapter Five: Why Popular Eschatology Needs to Be "Left Behind" — 83
    Timeline of "Rapture" Theology — 84
    Anabaptist Resistance to Dispensational Theology — 95

Chapter Six: Evangelicals, Anabaptists, and the Peace Challenge   **102**
    Evangelical Resistance to Nonresistance   103
    Anabaptist Resistance to Nonresistance   104
    Biblical Foundations of the Peace Position   105
    Christian Nonresistance   111
    A Cautious Digression   113

Chapter Seven: Evangelism – When We Go Fishing   **116**
    Evangelical Vision for Evangelism   118
    Evangelical Foundations for Evangelism   118
    Revival: The Evangelical Watchword for Evangelism   120
    Anabaptists and the Great Commission   123
    Combined Strengths   127

Chapter Eight: To Change the World –
Anabaptists, Evangelicals, and Political Involvement   **130**
    Anabaptist Anxieties Concerning the Powers   131
    Being Quiet Does Not Mean "Faithful"   134
    Were They Wrong?   135
    What Anabaptists Can Learn from Evangelicals   138
    An Evangelical-Anabaptist Matrix for Political Engagement   141
    One Example for Social Change   143

Chapter Nine: Reading the Bible Together
Through the Lens of Trust   **144**
    The Old Testament Testimony   146
    The New Testament Revelation   151
    A Hermeneutic of Trust   155

Chapter Ten: The Need for Evangelical and Anabaptist Cooperation   **156**
    Celebrating What We Have in Common   157
    Shared Struggles   158
    Why We Need Each Other   160

Epilogue: Merging but Not Emergent   **163**

Bibliography   **165**

THE ANABAPTIST
EVANGELICAL PUZZLE

Introduction

I am an Anabaptist.

What does that mean?

Like most labels, defining what it means to be Anabaptist requires sifting through the various definitions that have been applied to the term. In fact, a broad spectrum of faith-based movements identifies as Anabaptist. The markers vary as to what makes a group or an individual Anabaptist. When one of those markers becomes the stand-out feature of Anabaptism but we do not agree with it, we quickly distance ourselves from the brand that has been highlighted.

Consider, for example, that in my high school experience, one coarse fellow in our communications class identified Mennonites as those Bible-thumping people in black clothes riding on wagons. In a setting as volatile as high school in the 1980s, it was not healthy to disagree and present myself as the opposite of this ignorant declaration. He was the type who would use that confession against me and make my life miserable. Either I would be mocked as a "Menno" or persecuted as a Christian. Being relatively new in my faith, I am not sure I was ready for the latter.

More recently, a writer for a gospel network in Canada penned an article that cast all Anabaptists as somewhat heretical. He writes that Anabaptists are his friends, but that he must disagree with them and cites reasons why. Two mega-church pastors who come under the Anabaptist banner were the focus of this article and, thus, were set up as the typecast of all Anabaptists. One of these pastors promotes the value that Anabaptists believe in the Bible but follow Jesus. The other pastor held up the value of Christus Victor as the supreme perspective of the atonement of Jesus Christ.

While I agree with the basic values of these statements, I disagreed with the writer who placed all Anabaptists under the teachings of these two pastors. Somehow, these two men became the authoritative leadership of Anabaptists everywhere. I wrote to the author and told him that, as an Anabaptist, I would appreciate not being associated with these two men who have seemingly hijacked Anabaptist thought.

If I do not want to be culturally stereotyped as Amish or theologically pigeon-holed as a progressive Anabaptist, then what kind of Anabaptist am I? What kind of Anabaptist are you?

I Am a Mennonite

Contrary to the agrarian nature of most Mennonites of the last few centuries, I grew up in a modest-sized city. My parents were raised on farms but found work in the city at a time when there were not enough farms for everyone. The work in the city was appealing too. Despite the tenor of Mennonite preachers in the mid-twentieth century that cities were "dens of iniquity," many young families moved to the urban centers for work. Consequently, Mennonite churches sprang up in the urban centers of the Canadian Prairies to minister to and "sanctify" these urban Mennonites and keep them "holy."

A Mennonite without a farm is like a plow without a mule to pull it, or so it seemed to an urban Mennonite when meeting a rural Mennonite. How could you be Mennonite and not farm? It was as integral to our identity as faith in Christ was to our core values. What made us city-dwellers Mennonite?

The church, for one thing.

Our church was situated in the midst of an up-and-coming suburb of the city where a substantial number of Mennonite families had settled. Here in the foreign culture and influences of city-life was an island of refuge to which our families could flee on a weekly basis and be reminded of what made us different. We met to give our offerings in Sunday School, marvel at flannel-graph stories, meet friends, sing inspiring hymns, and listen to gospel messages—all in English, but more on that later.

On the sign outside our church were the words "Evangelical Mennonite Church." If I had known what I know now, I would have said our church was no different from the other evangelical churches in the neighborhood—except for one thing: when the adults visited, they sometimes slipped into speaking Low German, the language of the particular strain of Mennonites to which I am connected.[1] Otherwise, we dressed the same as anyone else and drove brand-spanking-new GM, Ford, or Dodge cars.

That Mennonite label on the sign gave me pause to wonder what it meant to be Mennonite. When my classmates in school would talk about their countries of origin, they talked about Germany, Ireland, India, and Botswana. I would say I was Mennonite as if it were a nationality. Other children looked at me like I was talking about a mysterious fictional country they had never heard about. I soon learned to say I was Russian, which I was not. Later, I deduced that I was

---

1 The stream of Mennonites to whom I belong are categorized as Dutch-German-Russian (DGR) following the flow of migration from the sixteenth century until the nineteenth century. Why we are we not called DGRC, as in Canadian, I do not know. The language known as Low German was the dialect of farmers and business owners who joined the Anabaptist movement in the Netherlands and Northern Germany in the sixteenth century.

Dutch until a man I met from Rotterdam told me he had never heard of the name "Klassen" in the Netherlands. Only in the last few years did I learn that my ancestors were from Westphalia in North-Western Germany. This lack of national identity only skims the surface of my confusion regarding my faith identity.

When I was around the age of eleven, our church's Sunday School department decided to try a different curriculum. They handed out a booklet to students that seemed to have been published by a Mennonite company. I began to read a narrative that stood out to me, which set me on a journey to discover what it meant to be Anabaptist.

I vaguely remember the entirety of the narrative, but I do remember the profound impact it had on me. In summary, the story focused on a family in an undefined time period, though I suspected it was a couple of hundred years ago. This family had been part of a state church in a nation that was also not identified, but they had become disillusioned with child-baptism and other practices. Finding like-minded followers of Jesus, they formed a group, a church of sorts, that met in the forest with rough-hewn logs as pews and only trees as the walls of their cathedral. There they worshiped God in freedom, baptizing those who believed and learning to follow Christ. I got the impression that they were not supposed to meet like this, that they were outlaws, and that getting caught would have serious consequences. The "outlaw" aspect was intriguing to an eleven-year-old. At some point in the narrative, a spy or a member-under-duress revealed the existence of this outlaw church to the authorities, and some of them were rounded up and taken to prison. Tension mounted and I was riveted to the narrative as I read voraciously, wanting to know what happened next. Some leaders of this "forest church" were tortured and killed, but the featured family clung to their faith and would not surrender to fear. These people were Anabaptists.

The distressing result of my story is that our Sunday School department never followed through in teaching this curriculum. I would have to wait several more years before I found out more about the Anabaptists in my Bible college courses. Christian Education in my Mennonite church, and I suspect in many others, was remiss in teaching this heritage of faith to the younger people. Maybe the directors felt the stories were too gory or frightening. Maybe they felt it was more important to be evangelical than Mennonite. One can only speculate, but as a result, many of my generation and younger have no idea what it means to be Mennonite or Anabaptist.

Muddying the waters further was the mixed message in my family home. My father was a twenty-something young man during World War II and followed the reports of the war very closely. He would regale me with anecdotes about how effective the Canadian army had been in the war, how the

Germans feared the Canadian soldier, and how important it was that "we" had won the war against Hitler. Add to this context the fact that my father, older brother, and I enjoyed watching war movies and westerns. These films served to exacerbate the myth of redemptive violence in my mind.2 I grew up believing that when the tyrant threatens, the gun is the answer. Some of my favorite westerns featured reluctant heroes who, when personally threatened, would take the abuse, but when loved ones were under the gun, they stood up to beat back the foe. *Shane,* starring Alan Ladd, fits that mold perfectly.

I went to schools named after war heroes and lived near streets named after soldiers or battles. My schools regularly presented services honoring the war dead on Remembrance Day. Every cultural influence in my little world exalted the myth of redemptive violence, and I bought it hook, line, and sinker. For the better part of my youth, I had no idea this ran counter to my Mennonite heritage.

Now the mud in the water: Sometime during the 1940s, my father was conscripted to fight on the battlefields of Europe during World War II. Resting on the exemption status from armed conflict accorded to the branch of Mennonites that settled in Western Canada in 1874, my father claimed conscientious objection. Upon his faith in Christ and the belief that Jesus would not want his followers to kill other human beings, dad stood before a judge and declared he would not fight. He was unashamed of his stand and often recounted those days. Though I respected my father's stand and never resented his choice, I grew up confused about how I was supposed to feel about war and redemptive violence.

For many Mennonites, the most glaring misunderstanding of our heritage involves our nonviolent stance. Without biblical exegesis and a proper understanding of the "peace position," many have rejected the position as being unrealistic in a violent world. If the peace position alone marks the Anabaptist-Mennonite as different from other churches, either the position is untenable or, more likely, preachers and Christian educators have not done a sufficient job of explaining all the core values of this faith perspective, including why we believe in peace over redemptive violence, in the person of Christ.

Mennonites have morphed over the centuries into a socio-cultural class of people and are known less for their radical faith in Jesus than their pe-

---

2   Walter Wink in his article, "The Myth of Redemptive Violence," describes how the belief that violence "saves" is so successful because it often appears to be true. Violence is so much a part of our world. Violence is the answer to many of the world's problems, or so it seems. It is the last and most effective resort in conflicts according to the dominant thinking of our age. Violence, however, contrasts everything that Jesus Christ came to do for humanity. The Bible in Transmission, Spring 1999.

culiar dress.[3] Even Mennonites today see themselves as a backward-looking race of people with conservative values that have often been stifling socially and theologically. Scores of churches have changed their street signs, taking the "Mennonite" out of their titles to change public perception and become more welcoming to the "non-Mennonite" who wants to worship in a local community church. While I do not agree with the philosophy behind the name-change, I do agree that Menno Simons, the founder of the Mennonite Movement, never intended for his name to be used as a label. Nevertheless, those who grew up Mennonite no longer want to be known as Mennonite and will attend other denominations or press for the name change.

In recent decades, it has become "cool" to be known as Anabaptist among those who have remained and for those who have discovered the true nature of the Anabaptist vision of church. The latter are often followers of Christ who either leave their church traditions and join an Anabaptist church or ascribe to Anabaptist values while working within their own denominations.

This brings us to the original question: What does it mean to be Anabaptist?

By the grace of God, the story of the "forest church" and my curiosity about the Mennonite faith led me to an Anabaptist Bible college. There, I began to discover that being an Anabaptist was not about the language one spoke, the food one ate, the clothes one wore, or the wagon one drove (or did not drive). Being Anabaptist was not about one's culture, in other words.

I Am an Evangelical

Here is another term that begged explanation in my youth.

Our church was part of a larger conference of evangelical Mennonites. In the middle of the twentieth century, it seemed good to the leaders of our brotherhood of churches to change the name of this collective from the German moniker to a brand that Canadians could understand. Having discovered the missionary fervor of the evangelical movement in the earlier part of the century, by the 1950s, it was in full swing. Adding "evangelical" to our Mennonite name expressed our desire to identify as a people who believed in evangelism and mission. This separated us from the Mennonites who had not yet understood the Great Commission Jesus had issued his followers. We *were now* evangelical.

How that evangelicalism manifested itself in our family was confusing insofar as to what it meant to be evangelical. My mother would challenge me

---

[3] Most North Americans envision an Amish lifestyle of plain clothes and horse-and-buggy transportation when they think of Mennonites.

in my childhood with an ethical dilemma and a guilt-induced conscience. For instance, I wanted to buy a comic book from a friend featuring Wonder Woman for a quarter. I had to ask for the money, so it was no simple task to convince my mother it was worth the coin. Her response was, "Do you think Jesus would be okay with you having this comic book?" (read: A comic book of a scantily clad woman who possessed power over men). On another occasion years later, I wanted to go to the movies to watch a Tarzan movie starring Bo Derek. Again, my mother posed a similar question: "Do you think Jesus would go to the movie theaters?" The supposition was that theaters were worldly and sinners congregated in those spaces.

My brother faced similar challenges. In his teens, he began hanging out with friends who smoked and drank. To my parents, these activities indicated a backsliding in faith; my brother was on the road to hell. The old familiar markers of sin—dancing, drinking, smoking, and attending venues of a worldly nature—were forbidden in our household as unbecoming of the Christian witness. Oddly enough, my siblings and I thought these prohibitions stemmed from being raised in a Mennonite home. In reality, I have discovered, these identifiers of what sin was originated in the evangelical tradition. Behind this evangelical mindset of what a Christian does and does not do was a fundamentalist influence that sought to guard against the sinful influence of the world.

Sidney Sheldon's book *In His Steps* posed the question, "What would Jesus do?" I believe my parents and other evangelical Mennonites took that question to heart. The question is valid, but it came to be used as a legalistic measuring stick to identify who was "in" and who was not living for the Lord. Many were shunned by church-going Christians who read their Bibles daily and abstained from vices, causing the less-than-righteous to feel they were beyond the grace of God. These lost sheep needed to be born-again, another term that gained popularity in the 1970s as a result of Charles Colson's book *Born Again*, an autobiographical book describing his conversion. This, too, was a measure of who the *real* Christians were in the world.

I do not fault my parents for their verve in wanting to give us a God-honoring, Christ-following home. My mother and father were products of the revival era of the 1940s and 50s, when traveling evangelists came to town and beseeched the multitudes to turn from sin and seek the mercy of a loving God. The impact on the hearts of thousands was amazing, and they did great things for Jesus. However, the baggage of guilt that accompanied the message of grace was so confusing. Perhaps in that era, the crowds needed to hear the kind of message that pricked the conscience, but the generation following heard only the guilt of not living up to a holy standard. We did not hear about grace.

Evangelicalism was in its purest sense a return to the New Testament call to preach Jesus and live a Christ-like life before our friends and neighbors. But in my world, in my church, among my peers, we had no clue what it meant to be evangelical except to avoid alcohol, cigarettes, and premarital sex. And the more we were told we should avoid these things, the more we wanted to find out why by tasting this forbidden fruit.

In my teens, when I discovered for myself the faith of my fathers in Jesus Christ, I began a long journey to understanding what it means to be evangelical and Mennonite. More than that, I am continuing to pursue Jesus and learn from him what true life is really like.

The Purpose of This Book

Being raised in an evangelical and Anabaptist environment, I am attached to both perspectives of the faith with their particular emphases. At times, I have found them to blend so well that I can hardly tell the difference theologically. Other times, glaring conflicts exist between the cultures of evangelicalism and Anabaptism. If we could extract the culture and put it aside, we may find even more common ground. But we are human, and we bring our history and our baggage with us into anything we do or think.

My aim in this volume is to contribute to the evangelical discussion from an Anabaptist perspective. Much criticism has been leveled at evangelicalism in the twenty-first century. These last two decades have been a soul-searching experience for many who have been disillusioned with the evangelical way of "doing" church. There are valid criticisms in that respect; some of mine will be obvious as you read ahead. Yet I also believe that evangelicalism must not be abandoned entirely; re-envisioned, yes.

Additionally, a great deal of ink has been expended on evangelicalism over the centuries; not much has been written about Anabaptism. The libraries do not need a lot of space to hold the Anabaptist tomes. My own branch of Anabaptism did not produce many writers in its earlier days. In fact, writers have only begun to spring up in the last fifty years. There is a dearth of sharing and processing through writing in the Anabaptist circles, especially in the theological sphere. I may not be the most qualified scholar to do so, but I pray these efforts will inspire others to write and share their perspectives.

I admit these chapters are entirely my own perspective, a product of my experiences and studies both in college and seminary and in the ministry. I do not pretend to have it all correct. This writing is but a chapter, if you will, in my own journey to understand the merging of evangelicalism and Anabaptism and how they work in my life.

These are not memoirs, however. The targets of this book include college students and those who have a like-minded yearning for clarity in their faith. Anyone can read this book; I write plainly. Anyone can critique this book; we live in an age of hypercriticism, as seen in the comments section of our social media or the ratings on Amazon. If you find this book is not for you, I will try not to be offended.

I try to address the major themes in Anabaptist-evangelical discussions in this volume. Admittedly, some may be missed or purposely left out. The themes that do garner attention are those that stood out as being critical to our understanding of faith from both streams. Given that the material researched for this book was originally for a seminary course in an Anabaptist track of studies, there will be a certain nuance.

Finally, I want to add my voice to the discussion. Bruxy Cavey and Greg Boyd have dominated the Anabaptist horizon as representatives of the Anabaptist perspective. If they are the faces of the new Anabaptism, it is our own fault as Anabaptists for not writing and speaking up. Anabaptists are notorious for being "the quiet in the land" and letting others do their talking. Putting my self-abasement aside, I want to offer up this book as a word of affirmation for the Anabaptist-evangelical coalition of thought and life.

Chapter One:
An Anabaptist Confession

Defining Anabaptism in a succinct and conclusive manner requires creativity and a forgiving spirit from the many chapters that identify as Anabaptist. Though the number of individuals and churches that come under that umbrella are relatively few compared to other branches of the global church, the variety of interpretations of Anabaptism are many. To begin to understand Anabaptism, one must return to the seed of this perspective of Christianity.

Anabaptism sprang from within the Reformation movement of the sixteenth century. In this respect, Anabaptism was dependent upon the pioneers of the Reformation and would not have emerged as a whole without the courageous efforts of individuals who took a stand for a living relationship with Christ against stifling tradition. Protestants and Anabaptists alike owe a great debt to the men and women who discerned the times and acknowledged that the condition of the church was critically ill.[4] Stories of courage borne out of faith in Christ abound as individuals filled with the Holy Spirit resisted the norms and traditions of the ailing church.

Among these pioneers of renewal in their Christian walk was a man named Peter Waldo (d. 1218). Waldo was the medieval version of Zacchaeus (Luke 19:1-10) who, when he met Jesus, resolved to give away much of his worldly goods and money. Zacchaeus had pursued money as the agent of life and happiness, cheating and alienating others through the business of collecting taxes to achieve his aims. Hearing that Jesus was coming to his village, his curiosity was piqued and he wanted to know this Teacher who offered a better way to live. When Jesus sought him out and offered to stay at Zacchaeus' house, his spirit was renewed through the acceptance and love Jesus offered him. Zacchaeus then pledged to give to those he had wronged and make right the relationships he had broken through greed. Jesus responded to Zacchaeus' act of charity by saying, "Today salvation has come to this house…" (9).

Waldo's experience parallels Zacchaeus in similar detail since he was a rich merchant in France who one day heard a traveling singer sing about a particular saint. Waldo came under deep conviction for his sins and sought out theological counsel regarding what to do with this conviction. Having received varying

---

[4] I differentiate between Protestants and Anabaptists because, while they are similar in many aspects of the faith, they differ in key theological areas. Protestants would have viewed being called an Anabaptist as slanderous.

answers and none that satisfied, he found one teacher who told him Christ's answer for the perfection he sought, "If you would be perfect, go and sell all that you have…" (Luke 18:22). Waldo went home and offered his wife the opportunity to keep whatever properties or items she wanted while he sold the rest and gave the money to the poor. He took very seriously and quite literally the words of Jesus in this regard and began to preach and teach in the streets. Having someone translate some of the New Testament into the local dialect, Waldo and those who now followed him took their message from town to town, spreading the gospel. The Waldensians, as they were called, believed the Sermon on the Mount held a special emphasis for living out the Christian life, and as a result, they were called the "Sermon on the Mount people."

John Wycliffe (d. 1384), often called "the Morning Star of the Reformation," urged that the Scriptures be made available to the common people in their own language. Until that time, only Latin translations were used in worship services, making the message of the gospel inaccessible to the uneducated. Wycliffe, a professor at Oxford University and an influential voice among the lords and people alike, began translating the Bible into English. The ecclesial authorities opposed this work saying, "By this translation, the Scriptures have become vulgar, and they are more available to lay, and even to women who can read, than they were to learned scholars, who had a high intelligence. So the pearl of the gospel is scattered and trodden underfoot by swine."

Wycliffe retorted, "Englishmen learn Christ's law best in English. Moses heard God's law in his own tongue; so did Christ's apostles." Wycliffe died of a stroke while in exile from his native England before the translation was finished. However, his friend John Purvey completed the translation, and its legacy impacts the world today. As John Foxe said in his book of martyrs, "Though they dug up his body, burnt his bones, and drowned his ashes, yet the Word of God and the truth of his doctrine, with the fruit and success thereof, they could not burn; which yet to this day…doth remain."

Another individual to whom Anabaptism owes a debt for paving the way was John Hus (d. 1415). Huss, a Bohemian priest with great preaching skills, inspired many of the Reformers and was one of the louder voices preaching against the indulgences offered by the Roman Catholic papacy.[5] Huss and his

---

5   An indulgence was a way to reduce the amount of punishment one had to undergo for sins. It could even reduce the "temporal punishment for sin" after death. The *Catechism of the Catholic Church* describes an indulgence as "a remission before God of the temporal punishment due to sins whose guilt has already been forgiven, which the faithful Christian who is duly disposed gains under certain prescribed conditions through the action of the church which, as the minister of redemption, dispenses and applies with authority the treasury of the satisfactions of Christ and all of the saints." Leading up to the Reformation, the selling of indulgences was a serious issue and they became, in our common understanding, a license to sin.

followers at the University of Prague were enamored with the writings of John Wycliffe and gave Huss a hunger for the Scriptures. While many were split over the status of Wycliffe as a heretic or a hero, Huss began to increasingly trust in the Scriptures. Church politics were becoming divisive, and the abuse of power was evident. The indulgences pushed the situation over the edge, and as Huss spoke out against the papal authority, he lost the support of his king. Not dismayed in the least, he wrote a treatise declaring that the true Head of the church was Christ alone and not the pope. In his conviction, to rebel against a greedy pope was to obey Christ. For this conviction, he would burn at the stake after his arrest and trial.

These short sketches of pre-Reformation heroes of the faith provide a foundation for the eventual emergence of a full-scale movement for reform within the church. Worth noting in every narrative is the desire to see the existing church become what Christ intended as opposed to splitting or dividing the church. Nevertheless, Anabaptists found in Peter Waldo the sincere desire to obey the Scriptures literally, and in Wycliffe and Huss the courage to disagree with the authorities that opposed Christ and take the consequences of their convictions. Like Waldo, the Anabaptists would be "Sermon on the Mount People."

Longing for reformation in the church came to a climax with the nailing of a paper full of "suggestions" to a church door in Wittenburg, Germany. Martin Luther (1483-1546), a monk and a teacher of Bible and theology at the University of Wittenburg, spearheaded the call for the church to find authority in the Word of God in contrast to the traditions of the ecclesial structure of the past centuries. They were more than suggestions, to be sure; Luther's 95 theses declared two central beliefs: that the Bible is the central religious authority and that humans may receive salvation only through faith in Jesus Christ, not by works.

The established church of that time wanted to maintain power and authority over the people, but that entailed keeping them in the dark about the reality of indulgences and the true message of the gospel. Luther's intention was to challenge the thinking of the time in an academic discussion; thus, he nailed his 95 theses to the church door on October 31, 1517. They would become the foundation of the Protestant Reformation.

The term "Protestant" finds its origin in Luther's protestation of Roman Catholic practices, specifically the indulgences and papal authority. Protestants reject the authority of the pope, both religious and political, and prefer to find authority for faith and life in the Scriptures. To ensure that those who followed his lead would live according to the authority of Scripture, Luther translated the Bible from Latin and Greek into German so that anyone with the ability to read could have access to the Scriptures.

Without question, the ancient church was in great need of correction. Luther, John Calvin, Ulrich Zwingli, and others pressed ahead with reforms as they deemed necessary. These Reformers issued a fresh and desperately needed call to return to the foundational narrative of Israel and her Messiah, Jesus Christ. Each Reformer, regardless of the differences they held, agreed that giving the common person access to the Bible to discover and realize their own faith and salvation apart from rituals was key to advancing the gospel of Jesus Christ.

According to the Anabaptists, the Reformers stopped short of fully embracing the needed change. Within a decade of Luther's famous stand, the Reformers chose political conservatism and were not willing to challenge their political sponsors. In some contexts, Reformers like Luther were backed and protected by the nobility of their regions. In the canton of Zurich, Switzerland, Zwingli had the support of the town council, and for fear of offending and losing the political currency he had achieved, he compromised on many of the critical concerns he once held. Unfortunately, the church had married the state under Constantine and needed a divorce from that relationship.

What came to be known as Constantinianism, the relationship of church and state began when Roman Emperor Constantine declared Christianity a legal religion early in the fourth century. Prior to this event, Christianity had been an outlaw religion, with many followers of Christ giving their lives for the faith at the hands of various authorities in the empire. Much blood was spilled, yet the church grew exponentially in those early centuries.

When Constantine was about to fight a critical battle that would give him the throne of the Roman Empire, he claims to have seen a sign in the sky: a bright cross with the words, "By this sign, conquer." Christ himself, according to Constantine, told him to take the cross as the emblem on his shields and standards. As a follower of Christ, Constantine wavered between complete submission to Jesus and the old pagan religions. This was likely a political rather than spiritual balancing act since the Empire was in transition. Christianity would not become the state religion until 381, forty-four years after Constantine's death. However, the course was set, and Christianity would become mired in the complex and dirty relationship with the state.

The Reformers would date the corruption of the church to the seventh century, around the time that the Roman Empire fell to barbarian hoards, whereas the Anabaptists clearly saw the soiling of the church in the fourth century. Many Reformers refused to admit that the signs of fallenness in the church to which they objected—the papacy, Pelagianism, hagiolatry, sacramentalism—were largely the fruit of Constantinianism: the confusion of the church and the world.[6]

A motivating factor for the Reformers maintaining the relationship between church and state was the power to effect the changes they desired. They sought to use the government officials, the political powers, and the nobility to enact their reforms. While the Reformers employed the state to empower church polity, the church consequently became an administrative branch of the state on the same level as the post office. If church discipline was administered in this paradigm, it would be administered by the police and the courts. Underlying this relationship was the belief in the invisible church.

The concept of the "invisible church" was a prominent theology attributed to Augustine of Hippo (354-430). Augustine was influenced by Platonism, the belief that true reality is invisible and that, if the visible reflects the invisible, it does so imperfectly. As such, the invisible church, the elect, are known only to God since the visible church is imperfect. Members of the invisible church are saved, while the visible church consists of some individuals who are either saved or unsaved. The Protestant Reformers used this concept to distinguish between the "visible" Roman Catholic Church, which was corrupt or imperfect, and those who truly believed. John Calvin believed that the invisible church was actually in God's presence and that only those adopted by grace as children of God were received into this church. Some of these elect are in the world, he said, but the elect included all those who were in Christ from the beginning of the world. In contrast, the church throughout the world was a large mixture of hypocrites who have nothing of Christ but the name and outward appearance.[7] Thus, using the state to do the work of the church was justified by the goal of transforming society and instilling Christian values on the populace, even by force if necessary. It would not matter if Christians-in-name-only were oppressed or at a disadvantage since the invisible church would not be adversely affected.

Reformers like Luther, Calvin, and Zwingli were correct to appeal to the Scriptures in renewing church polity. They were right to appreciate the divine ordination of the secular state. However, they did not take time to appreciate the dangers of continuing the church-state synthesis and its repercussions. Zwingli was inclined to move away from infant-baptism, for instance, but

---

6 *Pelagianism* is a belief in Christianity that original sin did not taint human nature and that a person has the capability to choose good or evil without the help of God. *Hagiolatry* refers to the idolatrous practice of worshiping the saints. *Sacramentalism* is the use of sacraments (bread and wine, baptism, etc.) as a means of saving activity. Thus, the taking of communion, or the Mass, will effectively provide the means for the individual to be saved from hell.

7 Institutes 4.1.7

compromised his convictions under pressure from the civil authorities. Without infant-baptism, the authorities replied, how will we know who the citizens of this canton are in the census?

The Anabaptists rejoiced in the work Luther had accomplished but called it a halfway Reformation. They also appreciated Zwingli's work but begged him to go further in his views of reforming the church. Anabaptist understanding of Scripture did not find a biblical basis for Luther or Zwingli's sacramental interpretation of the Lord's Supper or baptism. Furthermore, Anabaptists disagreed with Luther's definition of the church being wherever the gospel was preached and the sacraments administered. The church, the Anabaptists replied, consisted of true believers who voluntarily joined the church through adult believer's baptism. While Luther had indeed restored the gospel of grace, Anabaptists felt he should have broken with the state and ended the Constantinian relationship of church and state.[8]

The Anabaptist Vision Revisited

Out of the Reformation was birthed the Radical Reformation led by the Anabaptist wing of the church. Anabaptists broke with the Reformers, both Lutheran and Calvinist, by practicing adult-believers' baptism, as opposed to infant baptism. When the leaders of the Anabaptist movement sought to make this break, baptism was not the critical issue. The symbol of baptism represented the break rather than acted as the cause of the break. At the heart of the Radical Reformation was a desire to be completely obedient to the New Testament teaching for faith and life.

When the Anabaptists read the Scriptures, they could find no evidence for infant baptism, though other Reformers insisted it was a continuation of the Old Testament sign of circumcision. Following Peter's Pentecost sermon, the crowd was cut to the heart—convicted by the death and resurrection of Christ—and asked the apostles how they were to respond to this message. Peter's answer was, "Repent and be baptized every one of you in the name of Jesus Christ for the forgiveness of your sins, and receive the gift of the Holy Spirit." Anabaptist hermeneutics were simple in the approach to understanding the text. In this example, they interpreted the process of baptism as believe-repent-baptism, which an infant did not have the capacity to comprehend.

In respect to the New Testament, most Anabaptist groups advocated a literal application of Jesus' teachings. Like the Waldensians, Anabaptists were

---

8   Cornelius J. Dyck, ed. *An Introduction to Mennonite History* (Scottdale, PA: Herald Press, 1981), 36.

especially careful to adhere to the teaching of the Sermon on the Mount. Based on Christ's words in this sermon, Anabaptists rejected violence of any sort, oath-swearing, and the hoarding of material wealth. Positively, they also found in the Sermon on the Mount a basis for community, the voluntary church, and mutual aid. Taking the Sermon on the Mount seriously for the present life was a radically different approach than Luther or Calvin would teach. Protestant theology, for the most part, viewed the Sermon on the Mount as an ethic for the millennial reign when Christ comes again, and not at all practical or possible for the current era.

These differing views explain the varied approaches to discipleship among the Reformers. Luther, Calvin, and Zwingli took action to move the church out of stagnation and into a more vibrant and godly life in the Spirit and certainly made great strides in this respect. Anabaptists like Conrad Grebel, Felix Manz, Georg Blaurock, and Menno Simons, among others, offered a more radical critique of the church and the Christian life than Luther and the rest.

Harold Bender reflected upon the Radical Reformation in the mid-twentieth century and wrote this:

> The Anabaptists were concerned most of all about "a true Christian life," that is, a life patterned after the teaching and example of Christ. The reformers, they believed, whatever their profession may have been, did not secure among the people true repentance, regeneration, and Christian living as a result of their preaching. The Reformation emphasis on faith was good but inadequate, for without newness of life, they held, faith is hypocritical.[9]

While the tone of the above analysis appears ungracious, the testimony of the Reformers themselves reveals that Bender was not wrong. Luther and Zwingli taught that salvation was by grace through faith, an excellent departure from the works-based doctrine of the medieval Catholic church. However, it may be said that the teaching of grace alone may have contributed to a lowered spirituality among Protestants than when they were Catholic. In the same way that the sale of indulgences encouraged individuals to sin boldly with this get-out-jail-free card, as it were, grace without discipleship seems to have led down the same path. If we are saved by grace, Protestants surmised, what is the purpose of living a disciplined life?

---

9   Harold S. Bender, "The Anabaptist Vision," *https://www.goshen.edu/mhl/Refocusing/d-av.htm*. The Anabaptist Vision, given as a presidential address before the American Society of Church History in 1943.

Luther himself seems to have been aware of the trend toward a weakened discipleship. His hope five years after nailing the 95 theses to the Wittenburg door was that a true church could be established. Luther said, "We who at the present are well nigh heather under a Christian name may yet organize a Christian assembly."[10] However, only three years later, in December 1525, Luther and Caspar Schwenckfeld discussed the failure of this church to materialize. They had envisioned a New Testament church that would lead to the spiritual and moral betterment of the people but found instead very little change in the spirituality of the congregants.

Bender commented on the desire of Luther and his colleagues to establish such a church:

> Between 1522 and 1527 Luther repeatedly mentioned his concern to establish a true Christian church, and his desire to provide for earnest Christians (*"Die mit Ernst Christen sein wollen"*) who would confess the gospel with their lives as well as with their tongues. He thought of entering the names of these "earnest Christians" in a special book and having them meet separately from the mass of nominal Christians but concluding that he would not have sufficient of such people, he dropped the plan.[11]

In Switzerland, Zwingli found that establishing a "true church" was not politically and practically prudent. Perhaps the temptation to include the masses was too great; filtering out the nominal Christians would deplete the strength and the influence of the church on the community. Perhaps vanity played a part in declining to establish a New Testament church based on the strict adherence to the Word and discipleship; the more people in the church, the greater the perceived affirmation that Zwingli was right in his interpretations. In any case, Zwingli expected that the preaching of the Word and the administration of the sacraments was enough to produce the vibrant Christian life in the members of his flock.

Grebel and the Anabaptists, conversely, pressed Zwingli to establish a fellowship of true believers only. Taking this approach may seem elitist or exclusive to those who were unsure of their faith in Christ but wanted to explore the possibilities before committing oneself to the movement. "Exploring the possibilities" sounds very twenty-first century, and we cannot apply the in-

---

10 Karl Holl, *Gesammelte Aufs&aumltzezur Kirchengeschichte* (2nd and 3rd ed.) (T&uuml-bingen, 1923), 359.
11 Bender, *Anabaptist Vision*. See Luther's *Deutsche Messe*, translated in Works of *Martin Luther* (ed. C. M. Jacobs et a1.) Vol. VI (Philadelphia, 1932), 172, 173.

quisitive and commercial mindset to the sixteenth-century Christian. Either you were committed to being Anabaptist, Protestant, or Roman Catholic; there was no option to check "other" in that period of European history.

Joining the Anabaptists then, meant committing oneself to an outlaw life since neither the Roman Catholics nor the Protestants granted their movement validity, but persecuted them vigorously. It also meant committing oneself to the "Body of Christ" and all that this entailed. That which was missing from the Protestant cause, accountability to one another in the church, was a hallmark of Anabaptist life in the body of believers. One follower of Christ walked with another follower of Christ in mutual submission to the life of Christ. When one faltered or fell into the old sinful life practices again, the community of faith was there to rebuke, restore, and refresh the brother or sister who erred. This was one of the keys to succeeding where the Protestant church failed to be the New Testament church.

The Anabaptist Movement

What makes the Anabaptist Movement unique among other Reformation movements?

C. Norman Kraus summarized the Anabaptist Movement as follows: It was a radical, Jesus-centered, martyr movement.[12] Though Kraus wrote a summary of the Movement four decades ago, his definitions remain a constant and faithful source of reference for the person seeking to understand Anabaptism.

That the Anabaptist Movement was *radical* refers to its call for the complete revisioning of what it meant to be a follower of Christ as well as what it meant to be a member of society as they knew it at that time. Observers today might be tempted to call it a "revival," but the Anabaptists were not interested in reviving the existing structure. Their vision involved abandoning the Constantinian relationship of church and state as worldly and unbiblical, and to re-create the church according to New Testament values. They were not interested in change that would occur over several years or decades; they wanted change immediately, to become obedient to the Scriptures forthwith.

The Movement was also *Jesus-Centered*. Kraus wrote that the center of Anabaptist life and faith was Jesus, not the Bible and not church tradition. Evangelicals and Protestants today have expressed uneasiness about the centrality of Jesus over the Bible. They would agree that we all follow Jesus Christ and make him the focal point of our faith, but they wonder how a Christian can do this

---

[12] C. Norman Kraus, *Evangelicalism and Anabaptism* (Scottdale, PA: Herald Press, 1979), 173-174.

apart from the Bible. This is where some misunderstanding in the last decade has emerged about the Anabaptist perspective of Christ and the Bible.

To clarify, the Anabaptists took the Bible very seriously; Bible study was very important to these people. While the Bible was important to them, it remained a tool, an inspired witness to the person of Jesus Christ. They hoped to avoid "bibliolatry," which is the worship of the Bible, the elevation of the text to a point considered equal with God, or that studying the Bible is more important than a relationship with Jesus Christ. The temptation to treat the Bible as the fourth member of the Trinity is a real one for all Christians, no matter their tradition. Anabaptists agree with evangelicals who ascribe to Paul's declaration in 2 Timothy 3:16-17, "All Scripture is breathed out by God and profitable for teaching, for reproof, for correction, and for training in righteousness, that the man of God may be complete, equipped for every good work."

Where Anabaptists disagree with evangelicals is on the theory of biblical inerrancy. For a host of reasons, Anabaptists do not claim to be inerrantists, but they will not be discussed in this chapter. One key aspect related to Christocentricity will suffice: many who claim the Bible is inerrant will likewise claim the Word of God is problematic. The Bible is not the Word of God since Jesus Christ is the Word of God according to John 1:1. Make no mistake regarding the Anabaptist commitment to Scripture; they saw it as a reflection of Jesus and sought to obey His words no matter the consequences. As a result of their Christocentric focus, Anabaptists gave more weight to the Gospels than the rest of the New Testament.

That the person of Jesus Christ takes center stage of the Anabaptist movement does not make them unique. Lutherans, Reformed, and other Christian chapters of the church all agree that Jesus should be the central figure of the faith. The question of how he is made central creates the contrast between the denominations. Anabaptists view the Scriptures from the perspective of the centrality of Jesus Christ, for starters. All Scripture is interpreted from the standpoint of Jesus as portrayed in the Gospels. The Old Testament and the rest of the New Testament, the epistles and so on, are interpreted from the center point of the Gospels. As the Old Testament points to Christ, the letters of Paul, Peter, John, and others find their meaning in the person of Jesus.[13]

That the Anabaptist Movement was a *martyr* movement does not mean the Anabaptists went looking for persecution. The Greek word *martureo* means "witness," and Anabaptist historians say the Anabaptists were the first evangelists of the Reformation. Taken a step further, many would claim that Anabaptists were the true "evangelicals" of that day since they were true "gos-

---

13 Paul Lederach, *The Third Way* (Scottdale, PA: Herald Press, 1980), 19.

pelers." Their belief in the voluntary church, that one must choose to be baptized into the body of Christ as an adult, required a dynamic witness. They not only proclaimed their faith in Christ, but they also invited others into the life of discipleship. Since church and politics were so intertwined, even among Reformers, the Anabaptist proclamation drew the ire of the church in whatever state they happened to dwell.

If you were a German resident, the Lutheran church took exception; in Switzerland, the Reformed Church found the Anabaptists distasteful. When church and state were joined like this, being a resident of the state meant joining the state-sponsored church. Anabaptists were "citizens of heaven" and did not consider being a particular nationality to be any relation to their faith. As a result, the state church persecuted, even unto death, the Anabaptists who, thus, became martyrs for bearing witness to their perspective of Christ. Ironically, the people of these regions observed their courageous stand for Jesus Christ and joined them in throngs. Menno Simons, the Dutch Anabaptist leader, declared that this bold witness was "bearing the heavy cross of Christ" and "giving bold confession." In his estimation, persecution was a mark of the true church.

Finally, what is meant by the term *movement*? Anabaptists were like Luther and Zwingli in their hope that the existing church could be transformed into the body of Christ that the Scriptures envisioned. They were not trying to separate from the church and become a separate sect. When Grebel and his friends debated with Zwingli, they hoped only to bring clarification to issues of importance for the community of faith and discipleship. Where they saw error, they confronted it; where there was evil, they sought to separate from it; and when there was opportunity, they shared their faith. Anabaptists were a movement of people toward a defined set of goals, chief among them becoming like Christ. When Zwingli refused to be convinced of their arguments, the Anabaptists were left with no other alternative than to make a radical break with the main church in Zurich.

Core Values of the Anabaptist Movement

Another way to understand Anabaptist values is through the eyes of Harold S. Bender. In an address before the American Society of Church History in 1943, Bender presented what he called *The Anabaptist Vision*. Critics of Bender's definition suggest that he may have oversimplified the collective understanding of Anabaptism, but the address has nevertheless become a classic summary of Anabaptism. His paper provides a foundation, at the very least, for those who want to grasp the primary essence of the movement.

One of the core values held by Anabaptists, according to Bender, was discipleship or "the way of Jesus." The important word for the Anabaptists was not "faith" but "following" (Nachfolge Christi). In Charles Colson's book, *Born Again*, Colson described his own conversion using the biblical term from John 3:3, where Jesus told Nicodemus that in order to see the kingdom of God, you must be born again. That label became the identifier of true Christians as opposed to nominal Christians, Christians in-name-only. So prevalent was this usage that Jimmy Carter identified as "born again" when campaigning for the US presidential election in 1977, and won. However, while acknowledging the need for regeneration (new birth), Anabaptists recognized that the invitation "follow me" occurs more frequently in the Gospels than "born again." Even if the exact words "follow me" are not used, the reader of the New Testament can still discern that the impression of following Jesus has a stronger sense than being born again. Being regenerate is important, but what happens after you are born again? That was the concern of Anabaptists.

Following Jesus through obedience to his calling and example were of utmost importance to the Anabaptists. The Gospel according to John, which stresses the need for new birth, actually begins with a call to follow. John writes that two of John the Baptist's disciples follow Jesus when the Baptizer declares of Jesus, "Behold the Lamb of God!"[14] Andrew, one who follows after Jesus, invites his brother Simon to come and investigate this "Messiah." Jesus then finds Philip and simply says to him, "Follow me."[15] The Gospel of John concludes with similar invitations when, after describing Peter's death, Jesus again simply says, "Follow me."[16]

The impression we get from those two words "follow me" leaves no doubt that nothing less than imitation is required of the believer who dares to follow Jesus. More than imitation, following Jesus requires complete surrender to the person of Jesus of one's whole life. Jesus said, "If anyone would come after me, let him deny himself and take up his cross daily and follow me."[17] Following Jesus means the person who trusts in Jesus will die to self and possibly die literally for the sake of Christ. Dying to self will mean putting the priorities of Christ's kingdom ahead of one's own ambitions and priorities. It means being a servant to others in the same manner that Christ gave up his throne to become a servant and to rescue humankind by his death on the cross.[18] Anabaptists follow Jesus in this way because he is the revelation of how God meant for humankind to be and to live in this world.

---

14   John 1:36
15   John 1:43
16   John 21:19
17   Luke 9:23
18   Mark 10:43-45; Philippians 2:5-11

Menno Simons, the aforementioned leader of the Anabaptists in the Netherlands, chose as his banner verse 1 Corinthians 3:11, saying that Jesus is the only foundation for our lives. Hans Denck, a German teacher who was expelled from the city of Nuremberg for his "wild" ideas about baptism and communion, joined the Anabaptists after his expulsion. Denck's favorite saying was "No one can follow Christ except they follow him in life." For Denck, the imitation of Jesus counted more than the ceremony of church rituals. He saw baptism as the "covenant of a good conscience with God" and that inner baptism was more important than the application of water on the outer person.

Much more recently, Gareth Brandt commented in his blog,

> Baptism became a counter-cultural witness, a statement of allegiance to the kingdom of Christ rather than the kingdom of the world. In this sense, believers' baptism is really not the best designation of what the sixteenth-century Anabaptists died for. In fact, Arnold Snyder calls is "far too anemic a phrase" to describe the Anabaptist view of baptism. Baptist was not so much about belief or mental assent to a doctrine or creed, but rather it was the sign of a transformed life by a new birth of the Spirit and the commitment to following Jesus in all of life.[19]

At the heart of baptism for the Anabaptist was the pledge to follow Christ and to live one's life in such a way that it expresses one's citizenship in the kingdom of God. It was common practice in the sixteenth century to swear an oath to the city in which a person lived and worked. Anabaptists declined to swear such an oath because they had made their promise to God in baptism. Even though they were reviled for this stand, their ethic and lifestyle likely made them better citizens than some who swore the oath because they knew they were working for God and not the city masters.[20]

Another important core value for the Anabaptist Movement was that of community. At the heart of discipleship was living a life of love, which was all but impossible if not lived out in community with other believers. When the Enlightenment, also known as the Age of Reason, came upon the intellectual scene in the late seventeenth and eighteenth centuries, it brought with it the emphasis of the individual and one's rights as a human being. These were positive contributions to society to be sure, but the pendulum swung too far when individualism became more important than the community. If baptism incorporates people into the body of Christ, the community of faith, then the individual becomes accountable to the community of faith by virtue of this joining.

---

19 Gareth Brandt is a professor of theology at Columbia Bible College in Abbotsford, BC.
20 Colossians 3:23-24

This is where sixteenth-century Anabaptism responds to the seventeenth-eighteenth century rise of individualism that has reached ridiculous proportions in the twenty-first century. The Anabaptists called the voluntary commitment to community *Gallasenheit*, or submission to the body. As the believer submits to Christ, so the same believer also submits to the community of believers. An expression of submission reveals itself in how we love one another in the community of faith and how we allow ourselves to be loved. Part of this loving relationship is found in the uncomfortable confrontation of sin in the life of a brother or sister in the Lord. To correct or be corrected according to the discernment of the Scriptures expresses mutual love in profound ways that seldom finds manifestation outside of the community of faith if done properly and in the Spirit of Christ.

Both core values mentioned above may be found in the evangelical churches today that do not come under the Anabaptist umbrella. Many of the lines that separated Anabaptists from Protestants or evangelicals have blurred over the last century or so. However, one core value that stands out as uniquely Anabaptist is the Way of Peace. Evangelicals are loathe to accept this position as easily as they have the other core values. This resistance to nonresistance as a Christian alternative to nationalism or Constantinianism will be discussed later in the book.

Pacifism or Nonresistance was not held by all Anabaptists at the beginning of the movement. Early Anabaptists wanted to overthrow the ruling powers by force and establish a biblically oriented community. Two of these leaders, Jan Matthijs and Jan van Leiden, seized an opportunity to make the city of Muenster into a New Jerusalem on earth by force.[21] They were eventually slaughtered by the authorities after a drawn-out siege of the city. Menno Simons, among others, viewed these violent responses to societal ills as unbiblical and certainly not in keeping with the life of Christ that followers were to emulate. Violence must not be countered with violence, but with the peace of Christ, just as Christ responded to his enemies.

Even though the violent and erroneous Muenster Anabaptists failed to represent the Christ of the Gospels, they did have one doctrine correct—their belief that the kingdom of God was to be manifested in a historical place at a historical time. Believing that the kingdom of God would be physically manifested in a literal city was incorrect; believing that the kingdom of God was not future, but present and real, was moving in the right direction. Bender said, "The Anabaptist vision was not a detailed blueprint for the reconstruction of human society, but the Brethren did believe that Jesus intended that

---

21   Cornelius J. Dyck, ed. *An Introduction to Mennonite History,* 104.

the kingdom of God should be set up in the midst of the earth, here and now, and this they proposed to do forthwith."[22]

The kingdom of God does not come by coercion, or even political manipulation, for that would be contradictory to the pattern of Christ's reign and rule. No, the kingdom comes about as people of faith give themselves in submission to the way of Christ and to each other in community. "Repay no one evil for evil but give thought to do what is honorable in the sight of all. If possible, so far as it depends on you, live peaceably with all" (Romans 12:17-18).

An Honest Appraisal

To be fair to my own tradition of Christianity, I must offer an honest appraisal, especially in view of the critique forthcoming on evangelicalism. To be blind to one's own shortcomings leads to a triumphalism unbecoming to those who know there are warts on this visage. What are some detractors to Anabaptism that I have observed?

a) The quiet in the land – Anabaptists were severely persecuted in the sixteenth century, thousands dying for the stand that they took for re-baptizing adults. One can hardly blame the beleaguered little congregations for just wanting to experience peace. Unfortunately, over time and with a measure of prosperity in agricultural pursuits, they withdrew into a fortress mentality of self-protection. They sought to be holy, to be true to the Word of God as they understood it, but at the expense of not sharing the good news. Like a whipped puppy, the Anabaptist descendants—Mennonites, Hutterites, and Amish—hid under the chair, afraid to come out, afraid to express any view that would be considered radical. They became the "quiet in the land," a people who minded their own business and hoped that the governments they lived under would do the same.

b) Late to missions – Post-Reformation Anabaptists were tenacious in sharing their beliefs. Some would visit a town, preach or teach for a few hours, baptize several converts, and leave the same day for another town. Surprisingly, congregations sprung up out of this incredible zeal. But as mentioned above, the cost of this zeal was expensive and the heart for missional living was lost in the centuries of self-preservation.

All was not lost. Renewal for missionary zeal returned in the nineteenth and twentieth centuries at the same time as the evangelical fervor was sweeping

---

22   Bender, 54.

men and women into cross-cultural experiments in gospel-sharing. It is unfortunate that Anabaptists found their voice after a long period of silence, but they did eventually add their unique perspective to the Great Commission.

c) Cultural confusion – Being Anabaptist—particularly Mennonite, Hutterite, or Amish—one tends to confuse their faith with their culture. In the past, those who sought to join these fellowships were not assenting only to a unique belief in Christ but to a way of living, a culture formed around food and clothing.

Today, many have the impression that to be a Mennonite, you need to be born one. We speak of Mennonite food in my specific locale, which I often tell people is food derived (stolen) from the Ukrainians when we lived among them. There really is no such thing as "Mennonite" food. "Have you ever eaten a Mennonite?" quipped an acquaintance.

For the longest time, being Mennonite meant speaking a German dialect, working on a farm, and eating cottage-cheese-packed dough boiled in water. I grew up in a city, spoke only English, and only lately came to enjoy "that" food.

We have struggled, and continue to struggle, to convince those wanting to join our fellowships that "Mennonite" is a faith perspective, not a food you eat. To that end, many churches have discontinued using the term.

d) Obsession with peace – The greatest struggle of my own faith, and that of many Anabaptists or Mennonites, is understanding the commitment to peace. I have often found myself appreciating the justification for armed aggression, specifically in stopping the evil of National Socialism in the mid-twentieth century. Following World War II, many young Mennonites were convinced that if ever there was a just war, the war against Hitler must have been it. Inner turmoil was not assuaged, however, when we considered the great cost to life that resulted from this violence.

On the other side of the debate, Mennonites have clung to the doctrine of peace with such passion they nearly made a new religion out of peacemaking. Several leaders have commented that "peace is at the heart of the gospel." Justification for such statements arises from the belief that God wanted to make peace with humankind through the shed blood of Christ. While I agree with the sentiment in part, I believe the motivation for this sacrifice was the love of God, with peace as a fruit of the action. Love, ala John 3:16, compelled God to act on humankind's behalf to reconcile us to himself thereby creating peace. Yet some Mennonites are inclined to skip the motivator and worship "peace" as the be-all, end-all reason for our faith.

Are You an Anabaptist?

If "Anabaptist" means "re-baptizer," can followers of Christ claim to be Anabaptist? Those who have left their faith traditions to fellowship with Anabaptists, or even Mennonite churches, are not technically Anabaptist and neither are those who have grown up in Anabaptist or Mennonite churches. Having been baptized as adults negates the true meaning of the term. Those who have left infant-baptizing churches to join an adult-baptizing church, being baptized as adults on the profession of their faith in Christ, are true Anabaptists.

Obviously, using the term "Anabaptist" means something other than the literal designation just mentioned. Being Anabaptist means ascribing to the values that convinced the Radical Reformers to part ways with the Constantinian version of the church. It means making Jesus Christ central to one's life and practice and knowing him as the Scriptures have revealed him.

As many Mennonites leave their Anabaptist roots for other denominations of the church due to their critique of the cultural baggage and faulty works-salvation perception of the movement, those who have grown up outside this tradition are joining Anabaptist fellowships. What do Stuart Murray and Stanley Hauerwas see in the Anabaptist Movement that former Anabaptists failed to see? Is it possible the Anabaptist Movement possesses a five-hundred-year-old secret that the global church is only now beginning to appreciate?

Chapter Two:
Seeking Evangelical Fervor

Something has happened in the last decade or so to turn the stomachs of North Americans regarding the term "evangelical" in relation to Christianity. Many of us are unaware of what created the gradual distancing of even the Christian community regarding evangelicalism. Many writers point to the 2016 election of Donald Trump as president of the US as a determining factor, citing evangelical culture as "trumping" evangelical theology. Rational minds would opine that the election was merely the tip of the iceberg, the final straw indicating where evangelicalism in the US has finally landed.

Canadians have always been influenced by their neighbors to the south, politically, culturally, and, yes, theologically. The Religious Right and their political agenda have certainly left a bad taste in the mouths of Canadian evangelicals, but something more is at work in the growing disenfranchisement with evangelicalism. Putting one's finger on it has been a difficult effort, especially for those who know something is wrong but are not theologically or academically inclined to give it a voice.

Those in the pews of evangelical churches who have a penchant for a deeper analysis have stated that evangelicalism tends to put labels on people, stamping certain people as "in" and others as "out" of the true church. Evangelicalism has come to be known in that sense for what it is against rather than for what it stands. It bears a terribly close resemblance to the political advertisements on television where a political candidate spends all his or her time slamming the opposing party without telling the viewer what they intend to do when they come to office. Tell us something that will make life better, the potential voter cries. And so it has become with evangelicalism. This brand of Christianity has become known for being racist, judgmental, elitist, and homophobic.

One of the harshest criticisms of evangelicalism centers on the elitist proposition that evangelicals have a superior understanding of salvation. Indeed, many who have grown up in the evangelical tradition would probably confess that they were taught directly or indirectly to consider mainline denominations deficient in discipling their people toward a personal relationship with Jesus Christ. Their knowledge of salvation and the grace of God are tied up in tradition and ritual rather than in the evangelical truth revealed in Scripture, evangelicals say. Because evangelicals believe so strongly in their version of the gospel, they feel immense pressure, even guilt, when it comes to sharing the gospel with the unsaved. This leads to a "hard sell" evangelism that also pressures the unbeliever to make a decision "before it's too late."

These issues have given many Christians pause to reconsider the value of being called evangelical in today's cultural climate. One fellow remarked that he "broke up" with evangelicalism and subsequently felt a great release from the associated pressures of that position or label. Another person wondered whether Jesus himself would have identified as evangelical since, this person opined, Jesus was not really into labels.

In respect to these concerns, does the church today need to abandon the term "evangelical"? Has it been hijacked by the Religious Right in the US and tainted so detrimentally that it can no longer be used to describe Christians? Have evangelicals forgotten what it means to be evangelical, or can they reclaim the adjective to describe an ardent fervor for the truth and grace of Christ?

What It Means to Be Evangelical

Investigating the true meaning of "evangelical" might make it difficult to divorce the word from current usage despite how it has been hijacked. It may need to be wrested back from those who have misused the term. "Evangelical" comes from the Greek word *euangelion*, which in Latin is *evangelion*. We translate the term as "gospel" or "good news."

Euangelion, as a term, could mean simply "good news," as in how the Septuagint used the word in 2 Samuel 4:10: "When a man told me, 'Saul is dead,' and thought he was bringing **good news** [εὐαγγέλια], I seized him and put him to death in Ziklag." Roman writers also used the term to refer to religio-political reality when applied to Caesar Augustus:

> It seemed good to the Greeks of Asia, in the opinion of the high priest Apollonius of Menophilus Azanitus: 'Since Providence, which has ordered all things and is deeply interested in our life, has set in most perfect order by giving us Augustus, whom she filled with virtue that he might benefit humankind, sending him as a **savior** [σωτήρ], both for us and for our descendants, that he might end war and arrange all things, and since he, Caesar, by his appearance.... surpassing all previous benefactors, and not even leaving to posterity any hope of surpassing what he has done, and since the birthday of **the god** [τοῦ θεοῦ] Augustus was the beginning of the **good tidings** [εὐαγγέλιον] for the world that came by reason of him...[23]

---

23 This text is tagged OGIS 458 / SEG IV no 490, which means that you can see more about it in *Orientis Graeci Inscriptiones Selectae* (a 1905 compilation by Wilhelmus Dittenberger usually abbreviated as OGIS, available online) or in *Supplementum Epigraphicum Graecum* (SEG) volume 4.

In other words, the Greeks grew weary of the discord in the known world, and when Augustus brought peace to the political scene, they revered him as god and savior. As Roman legions entered new territories and took control, they proclaimed the "good news" of the Empire. If the populace accepted this new world order, then the peace and prosperity the new regime presented as potential seemed like "good news." "A gospel is an announcement of something that has happened in history, something that's been done for you that changes your status forever."[24]

New Testament writers adopted *euangelion* to declare the best news the world had yet heard and would ever hear. Paul declared this gospel not as a scheme of soteriology, not as a new religion, and not even as a teaching of justification by faith but as the message of the crucified and risen Jesus of Nazareth. Move aside, Caesar, the true King and Lord has entered the scene, and the Jewish Messiah—the Isaianic prophecy of Yahweh's servant, the Son of God— has set the captives free. The Roman gospel met the Christian gospel and has been overturned.

Just as the Roman procurators, legionnaires, and diplomats brought the Imperial good news to the world, the apostles of the early church were ambassadors of the good news of Christ to the world. Thus, the apostles were the first true evangelicals in the history of the church, proclaiming the good news and writing Gospel accounts to herald the Lord's new world order. The apostles were the first heralds of the Christian faith.

Fast-forward to the Reformation, both Protestants and Anabaptists thought of themselves as evangelicals because they taught that salvation was by grace through faith. Whereas other Christian traditions were teaching a works salvation, the Reformers rediscovered the New Testament doctrine of grace and rejected merit-based religion. Anabaptists went still further, in their estimation, by returning to the model of the New Testament church and, more specifically, taking the words of Jesus literally. Both were heading in the same direction so that, for the sake of argument, Protestant and Anabaptist movements were indeed evangelical.

Martin Luther professed to preach an evangelical account of salvation in Christ and, by doing so, drew the proverbial line in the sand against the Roman Catholic Church, which he considered corrupt. "Evangelical," as a descriptor of Luther's preaching, contrasted a faithful proclamation of the New Testament gospel message over and against Catholic perversions of that message.

Evangelical came to stand for:

---

24 Timothy Keller, *King's Cross* (New York, NY: Dutton, 2011), 15.

- Justification by faith, as opposed to trust in human works as the path to salvation.
- Christ alone as sufficient for salvation, as opposed to human mediations of the church.
- The once-for-all triumph of Christ's death on the cross, as opposed to the repetitive ritual of Christ's sacrifice as expressed in the Roman Catholic mass.
- The final authority of the Bible as read by believers, as opposed to what the Catholic priest told the people it meant.
- The priesthood of all believers, as opposed to the reliance on a class of priests ordained by the church.[25]

The for-and-against nature of the above description was unavoidable since the reformers were reacting to the injustices and failings of the existing establishment. More positively, evangelicalism professed a belief in the Trinity; the Bible alone as the Word of God; salvation by grace alone through faith; and that Jesus Christ is the Son of God in the flesh, and his death and resurrection were the answer for human sin. To be "evangelical" does not mean one belongs to a particular denomination but identifies a person or group as embracing these truths.

The Response of Fundamentalism to Religious Liberalism

If the narrative of evangelicalism found a definitive definition in the Reformation alone, we could close the file on this discussion. However, evangelicalism continued to find definition in the events of history, including the Enlightenment and the rise of liberalism. Modern evangelicalism arose out of fundamentalism which in turn was a response to liberalism.

Liberalism is an umbrella term for the developments in Christian theology and culture since the Enlightenment of the late eighteenth century. It has become mostly mainstream within the major Christian denominations in the Western world. Liberalism served as an intellectual reaction against the conservative Protestant traditions that dominated the North American and some European contexts. In particular, liberalism attempted to answer the

---

25 Mark Noll, *The Rise of Evangelicalism* (Downers Grove, IL: InterVarsity Press, 2003), 16-17.

evangelical doctrines of the supernatural character of Christianity, the Bible, and salvation with science and reason.

Grant Wacker explains the thrust of this movement in his essay "Religious Liberalism and the Modern Crisis of Faith." In summary, he writes that religious liberalism attempted to reconceive the essence of Christianity in the face of powerful intellectual challenges that had been stirring in educated circles since the mid-century. For example, the recognition and growing consciousness of **other world religions** [how do we know that we have the only true faith?]; the **rejection of "Young Earth Creationism"**; and acceptance of scientific theories such as **Darwin's Evolution** [natural processes proceeded at random, without any hint of divine direction]. These theories seemed to undercut the authority of the Bible and suggest that Christian morality was nothing but a convenient survival mechanism. Liberalism also introduced the science of **biblical higher criticism** that developed questions of authorship, such as who wrote the various parts of the Bible? How did those authors reflect the assumptions and prejudices of their cultural times? This approach to the Bible further presupposed that the Scriptures could, indeed must, "be understood as any other ancient text, without recourse to the supernatural explanations." Eliminating the supernatural from the scholarly discussion of how the Bible came to be the Bible became the chief mark of liberalism and the greatest point of contention with conservative scholars.[26]

Furthermore, liberalism rejected penal substitutionary atonement and supernatural conversion. Underlying this position was the belief that human beings were essentially good and that society and culture were evolving and getting better as history moved along. As a result, liberals believed humankind was progressing toward a utopian existence through rational, dedicated human effort.

American fundamentalism emerged as a response to theological modernism (liberalism) in the 1920s. Fear of losing congregants to modernist ideas, fundamentalism battled with liberalism in the academic institutions and denominations. Fundamentalism insisted upon the authority of the Bible for every aspect of life, including the origins of our universe and behavioral ethics based on the belief that the Bible was inerrant. Proponents of this response to liberalism reasserted the supernatural character of the new birth, thereby insisting on the need for spiritual regeneration. Salvation by religious conditioning was an impossibility given the sin nature of all human beings, they said. If the Bible is inerrant, the practical outworking of this stance demands that it be taken literally, which they did.[27] In keeping with this stance, funda-

---

26 From Grant Wacker, Duke University Divinity School. "Religious Liberalism and the Modern Crisis of Faith" http://nationalhumanitiescenter.org/tserve/twenty/tkeyinfo/liberal.htm.
27 C. Norman Kraus, *Evangelicalism and Anabaptism*, 10.

mentalists also accepted the Plymouth Brethren concept of the dispensational interpretation of Scripture and essentially adopted the Scofield Bible (1909) as their main translation of the Scriptures. Consequently, their view of eschatology was a literal reading of apocalyptic literature and the kingdom of God was a future event.[28] Personal salvation, while given greater emphasis, focused on getting ready for the kingdom rather than living in it in the present.

Reacting to liberalism instead of firming up the foundation for a reasonable faith made fundamentalism into a separatist or sectarian movement. In other words, they adopted a fortress mentality and retreated into their "safe" zones, being suspicious of anyone who did not share their "fundamentals." One could say they were known more for what they were against than what they stood for in the world.

Fundamentalism lives on today, as do some forms of liberalism. Some readers will applaud the stand fundamentalists took to defend the Christian faith and the authority of the Bible. Other readers will scoff at the backward approach fundamentalists took toward science and reason, especially when considering the so-called Scopes Monkey Trial in 1925 and the untenable position of biblical inerrancy.[29] Could science and reason co-exist in the realm of religion together with the orthodox position of conservative theology? Fundamentalists in that generation said no. But how long could a movement continue based on a platform that was against higher learning and reason and a populace that demanded a more informed answer than "just have faith"?

The Rise of Popular Evangelicalism

Following the Scopes trial and other "defeats" of the 1920s and 30s, modern evangelicalism arose out of a desire of various Christian leaders to distance themselves from the anti-intellectual, militant, culture-shunning traits that had become fundamentalism. Evangelicalism, in this early stage of its existence, began as being *for* the gospel instead of *against* various so-called threats to Christian orthodoxy. So, in 1942, the formation of the National Association of Evangelicals (NAE) initiated a movement toward developments in conservative Protestantism. The movement rejected the Federal Council of

---

28 C. Norman Kraus, *Evangelicalism and Anabaptism*, 12.
29 The Scopes Monkey Trial was a highly publicized court case that prosecuted John T. Scopes for teaching evolution in a high school, which was illegal in Tennessee. Scopes merely symbolized the greater contest that was brewing between fundamentalists and modernists, which set modernists, who said evolution was not inconsistent with religion, against fundamentalists, who said the Word of God (the Bible) was superior to all scientific theory. The fundamentalist position, headed by William Jennings Bryan, was publicly damaged by the trial since it revealed academic ignorance on the part of fundamentalists.

Churches and the American Council of Christian Churches because of their fundamentalist and separatist leanings. Instead, the NAE called for a unified, dynamic, and cooperative set of programs focusing on evangelism, Christian education, missions, and politics based on traditional evangelical beliefs.

In a surprising move, the NAE statement of faith left "biblical inerrancy" out and chose instead to use the term "verbal and plenary" inspiration. By "verbal," they meant every word of Scripture is given by God; by "plenary," they meant every part of the Bible was equally authoritative; and by "inspiration," they meant God supernaturally guided the biblical authors to write precisely what God wanted them to write.[30] The NAE recognized that not every narrative or event was morally proper. For instance, when Joab murdered Abner (2 Samuel 3:26-30), the reader should not understand that such actions were divinely authorized as a prescription for life. Verbal plenary inspiration applies to the original manuscripts, also known as autographs, which the NAE believed were written by the prophets and apostles as God divinely directed them. Today, the church possesses imperfect copies of perfect originals, according to the NAE. This position on the Bible does not allow for mistakes in historical events or locations or, more significantly, the personality of the author to influence the text with his or her idiosyncrasies.[31]

Even though superior terminology and a greater grace in respect to the authorship of biblical texts begs to be employed, the NAE, to their credit, was trying to demonstrate a spirit of tolerance within the evangelical boundaries. To that end, they omitted any reference to the premillennial interpretation of the second coming of Christ; they strove for spiritual unity among the believers; and moved toward cooperation in parachurch ministries. Emerging from this effort were organizations like Youth for Christ (1944), the Evangelical Foreign Missions Association (1947), the Evangelical Theological Society (1949), and the Billy Graham Evangelistic Association (1949), to name a few.

Modern Evangelicalism's Appeal

When the modern evangelical movement gained traction in the late 1940s, it possessed a mass appeal for many North Americans who were looking for a vibrant faith. This vibrancy carried the movement on for several decades and only began losing its fervor toward the end of the twentieth century. What was so appealing about this brand of evangelicalism?

---

30 "What Is Meant by the Verbal Plenary Inspiration of Scripture?" Blue Letter Bible. Accessed March 6, 2019. https://www.blueletterBible.org/faq/don_stewart/don_stewart_416.cfm.
31 C. Norman Kraus, *Evangelicalism and Anabaptism*, 12.

For one thing, the message was simple. Many evangelical pastors adopted a "how-to" approach to preaching on Sunday morning. They would take the text or, more likely, several texts, and develop an outline of three keys, principles, or challenges that told people how to live out their faith in the coming week. Pastors did not normally delve into the background of the passages, looking for context or ancient cultural cues that just may change the meaning of the text, or expound on the classics of post-Nicaean theologians. Their task was simple and not at all analytical since the congregation was not theologically trained either and did not need a "deep" message. Evangelical hermeneutics in those decades was straightforward and even a bit black and white. The aim of evangelical preaching was to be understood. Lawrence Burkholder offered a critique of this style of preaching, saying, "Remarkably little Bible content is to be found in evangelical preaching. There are numerous references to the Bible as the Word of God, but seldom is the Bible exposited thoroughly and thoughtfully."[32]

There were, to be fair, exceptions to the above-stated critique. Dr. Martyn Lloyd-Jones and Ray Stedman were among the dedicated evangelical pastors who carefully exposited the Scriptures. However, most congregants were drawn to charismatic personalities who emulated the Billy Graham style of passion and fury at sin. Until Bible colleges became the popular destination of young adults in the latter decades of the twentieth century, most congregants were drawn to the storyteller and the passionate gospeler. As post-secondary education increased in availability to young adults, the congregations began to hunger for an intellectually stimulating and exegetical message. Suddenly, pastors needed to step up their own academic and theological pursuits to meet the demand for "meatier" messages.

Another related quality of evangelicalism that appealed to the masses was its evangelistic zeal. Evangelicalism brought to the fore the urgency of "winning the lost," a biblically motivated plan of evangelism. In the early decades, post-World War II, preachers were still pounding the pulpits about the fires of hell. That carried on for a short time until preachers realized the men who came home from the war felt they had been to hell (on the battlefield) and they could no longer scare them into heaven.

Evangelicalism rightly began proclaiming the forgiveness of sins and the love of God in Christ. Congregants were soon equipped to personally venture out and engage in friendship-evangelism. Some were armed with the "Four Spiritual Laws" or the "Roman Road," memorable mantras for sharing the

---

32 J. Lawrence Burkholder, *Evangelicalism and Anabaptism*, "Ch. 2 Popular Evangelicalism: An Appraisal," 32.

gospel with anyone they met.[33] As a whole, evangelicalism utilized TV and radio broadcasts, crusades, special outreach events (films with evangelistic themes; concerts), and evangelistic campaigns ("I Found It" and "Power to Change," both by Campus Crusade).

The fervor of evangelicalism in spreading the good news had a positive effect on other Christian movements, including Anabaptism. So, despite some misguided and "in-your-face" moments where the "born-agains" became obnoxious, the intent to share Jesus Christ was correct. Anabaptists benefited from the evangelical influence, as did other faith traditions.

Finally, evangelicalism appealed to the masses because of its "individual" emphasis. One cannot help but note the irony of appealing to the masses concerning their individuality, but precisely because the Enlightenment began to focus on the singularity of personhood, the fruit of this ideology was the heightened sense of self. Prior to the mid-twentieth century phenomena of the "me" generation, people were content to be identified with ethnic groups, family circles, church denominations, and other associations. Now a person wanted to feel that he or she alone mattered. Evangelicalism answered this need by emphasizing that the individual was specifically known and loved by God and that God had a special interest in him or her. Women and men could take the words of the Bible personally and have an intimate relationship with him. Nothing else offered a personal connection with the Holy Other, the Transcendent One, quite like the good news as proclaimed by the evangelical community.

An Appraisal of Modern Evangelicalism

Evangelicalism has come under fire in the last decade or so, and the criticism comes not just from the outside, but from disillusioned evangelicals as well. David Fitch offers a critique of evangelicalism in his book *The End of Evangelicalism* in which he says,

As we look at evangelicalism as an ideology, we must also ask whether some of our most basic beliefs and practices have become soothing ideologies. Far from calling us into a gospel faithfulness, have our beliefs become the

---

33 The Four Spiritual Laws is the title of an outreach booklet created by Campus Crusade for Christ founder Dr. Bill Bright. The Four Spiritual Laws in brief are 1) God loves you and created you to know him personally; 2) Man is sinful and separated from God, so we cannot know him personally or experience his love; 3) Jesus Christ is God's only provision for man's sin. Through Him alone, we can know God personally and experience God's love; and finally, 4) We must individually receive Jesus Christ as Savior and Lord; then we can know God personally and experience His love. The "Roman Road" is a select number of verses from the book of Romans that can also be used to lead a person to faith in Christ.

means to maintain the status quo while at the same time comforting us that we still believe?[34]

Fitch identifies and evaluates three specific signifiers of evangelicalism people give their allegiance to, which mark them out as belonging to the movement: belief in an inerrant Bible, the decision for Christ, and the ideology of the Christian nation. This next unit will look at these three and other signifiers that convince evangelicals they are indeed evangelical, but which may constitute a false sense of security.

a) The Inerrant Bible: Belief in the inerrancy or infallibility of the Bible rises from a high view of Scripture among evangelicals. That they have committed themselves to the authority of the Bible as the authority for life and faith is praiseworthy. However, the average evangelical congregant may scarcely be able to define what biblical inerrancy means. Yet they know the Bible is completely trustworthy, and any talk of error in the original manuscripts is heretical.

We have already discussed how the doctrine of inerrancy arose as a response to the fundamentalist-modernist controversies of the 1920s and 30s. Modernist professors and pastors within mainline Protestantism were teaching the higher criticism of the Bible, that the Bible was fallible and contained many errors.[35] Higher criticism was employed as a term to denote the study of the historic origins, dates, literary structure, and authorship of the books of the Bible. Every teacher and pastor worth their titles wants to find out all they can regarding the passage of the Bible they are studying, such as the author, context, date, and purpose for its writing. However, the fundamentalists were concerned about the subjective conclusions with which some critics began their criticism of the biblical text. Once they found a dubious basis for an author's style or literary qualifications, the critics questioned the authority of the text and the value for spiritual growth. If the critic comes to the biblical text without faith and without reliance on the Holy Spirit, he has no revelation to make to the unbiblical mind. Higher criticism, though necessary to the study of the Bible, could also be faith-shaking for those on the edge of doubt.

An example of higher criticism that shakes the supporting pillars of the average evangelical congregant is found in a study of the letter to the Ephe-

---

34 David Fitch, *The End of Evangelicalism* (Eugene, OR: Cascade Books, 2011), 24.
35 Mainline churches include the so-called "Seven Sisters of American Protestantism"—the United Methodist Church, the Evangelical Lutheran Church in America, the Presbyterian Church (USA), the Episcopal Church, the American Baptist Churches, the United Church of Christ, and the Disciples of Christ—as well as the Quakers, Reformed Church in America, African Methodist Episcopal church, and other churches.

sians. Most readers assume Paul wrote the letter. A closer study reveals that the grammatical style and literary structure do not match Paul's usual pattern of writing. Couple this with the oddly similar letter to the Colossians and critics have concluded that Paul wrote Colossians, but not Ephesians. Without diving into the minutia of evidence for this conclusion, doubting Paul's authorship of the letter to the Ephesians is enough to create havoc in the reader's heart and mind.

To protect their congregants, fundamentalists responded with the "inerrancy doctrine" that affirms the statement of their faith: "We hold the Scriptures to be infallible and inerrant in their original autographs." Successors to the fundamentalist movement, evangelicals adopted this position for the most part, though they did prefer the aforementioned "verbal and plenary inspiration."

Believing in the inerrant Bible does very little in assisting evangelicals to interpret the Bible for practical discipleship. If the Bible is inerrant, this allows the reader to interpret the Bible to mean anything they want it to because it is, after all, inerrant.[36] The reader can take any text—for example, Jeremiah 29:11— and claim its promise of prosperity and success. No one can dissuade them from their interpretation because the dissenter would be questioning the orthodox understanding of Scripture.

Evangelicals, then, are dabbling with over-spiritualizing the Bible, treating it as a book of magic. The discipline of reading the Bible and praying every day speaks of great intentions but runs the risk of instilling guilt in the person who fails to do so every day. When a crisis arises, many evangelicals have assumed the cause was the omission of personal devotion time in Bible reading and prayer. The fear is that "My day just won't be blessed if I miss my devotions." A healthy commitment to Bible reading and prayer is not being criticized in this evaluation; rather, the superstition and mystique surrounding Bible reading bear criticism.

Again, the positives of daily Bible reading and memorization cannot be emphasized more strongly in evangelical circles. Where evangelicals go awry is in their attitude toward these practices. Memorizing Scripture makes one familiar with biblical truth. Verses taken out of context and used for personal claims, however, lead many astray. Using Scripture to ward off bad feelings comes close to chanting magical incantations. Is it the verse or the faith in Christ that protects the speaker?

Finally, Billy Graham, the fiery evangelist of the mid-to-late twentieth century, popularized the expression "the Bible says…," which assumed this

---

36 David Fitch, *The End of Evangelicalism*, 54-55.

alone was enough to authorize what he said next.[37] Many preachers followed Graham's example and believed their congregations would submit to that expression out of reverence for the inerrant Bible. A true evangelical was expected to accept whatever principle or key thought was presented from the pulpit as authoritative. Unfortunately, this attitude leaves little room for discernment and being "good Bereans" in regard to preaching.[38]

b) The Decision for Christ: As a signifier, the "decision for Christ" became a major marker for evangelicals in determining if someone was a true believer. Asking someone if they had made a decision for Christ was the same as asking if they were "born again," or seriously following Jesus. It identifies evangelical belief and allows a certain measure of security and comfort in knowing that this person "believes what I believe." True fellowship between true believers can only be had on this basis, or so evangelicalism has taught us. Anyone who deviates from this pattern is, again, suspect.

"Knowing your spiritual birthday" was based on the idea that making "the decision" to be born again was as significant as being born the first time. To be sure, being saved from sin ought to be an important event, but to have forgotten the day was tantamount to a lack of assurance in evangelical circles. The stress on knowing the date of one's decision was so great that if the person was unsure of when they were "saved," that person may be encouraged to pray again and mark down the date. Readers may quickly recollect that they, or people they know, have never made a definite decision to follow Christ, but have, somehow, always known Christ and have followed him as a normal course of living. These folks, for the most part, have grown up in Christian homes, being taken to church and raised with Judeo-Christian ethics by their parents. For them, the decision is moot because there was never a day they did not think to include Christ in their lives.

However, evangelical pressure to "evangelize" children forced parents to say the "sinner's prayer" with their youngsters as soon as they could talk and understand certain concepts of sin and remorse. Many baptismal testimonies began with "I was raised in a Christian home" and added being saved at the age of five years of age, generally speaking. Just as often, these testimonies include falling away from that decision in the teen years, followed by a renewal or rededication of faith. How many made the decision at five years of age and did not come back to Christ would make a sad but important survey, to be sure.

---

37 Fitch, 48.
38 Acts 17:11 – "Now these Jews were more noble than those in Thessalonica; they received the word with all eagerness, examining the Scriptures daily to see if these things were so."

Dwight Moody said, "I look upon the world as a wrecked vessel. God has given me a lifeboat and said, 'Moody, save all you can.'" Many crusades and revivals have operated on this principle in the last century, giving rise to the term "lifeboat evangelism." Of the thousands who made decisions to live for Christ at crusades, 3 percent attended church after the experience. Attending church should not be considered the litmus of a true believer, but the statistic reveals the level of commitment "the decision" has borne in the individual. Some evangelists have even admitted that upwards of 25 percent of those making decisions at crusades were already "born again." The emotional appeal of sermons at these events had that kind of effect on even the most committed Christians.

Aside from the emotional manipulation inherent in the evangelistic crusade, the Moody quote reveals a deeper theological issue: escapism. The lifeboat analogy suggests the world is a sinking ship and the only way out is through believing in Jesus. One of the predominant questions at crusades or in certain evangelistic techniques is, "Do you know where you are going when you die?" Prompted by fear, the hearer trembles with the realization that he or she does not know what will happen when death comes and makes "the decision." Evangelists push the judgment of "sinners in the hands of an angry God" and offer the only escape through the grace of God in Jesus. Escapism's main fault rests in its future hope and provides no answers for the present dilemmas the average person faces. How does the good news of Jesus change a person, a community, or the world in the here and now?

Still, the evangelical evangelist persists, "Do you know where you are going when you die?" We want to be assured that in the event of our death, we will be secured a place in the afterlife. But does the tactic truly offer the personal assurance it sells? Do we really know where we are going? Can anyone testify to their success in attaining the experience of life after death? These questions do not create doubt; they reveal the doubt that lingers in the mind of the convert after the decision has been made. The convert will begin to wonder if she was sincere when she made her decision. She may wonder if the "sinner's prayer" took effect; was it enough? No one knows the answers to these questions until they die. A verifiable phenomenon of these doubts manifests itself in the multiple visits to the altar when the invitation to receive Jesus is given. Maybe this time she will feel the change, the difference Jesus makes, or the peace she seeks in confessing her sin.

Basing true belief on "the decision" reveals a faulty understanding of what it means to have faith in Christ. If faith were a simple matter of reciting the "sinner's prayer," then the rich young man need not have given up his wealth to enter the kingdom of God.[39] Many who prayed this prayer are considered "in" by virtue of the prayer and not so much on the evidence of a changed life. Getting someone to make the decision and pray the prayer has been the primary focus of evangelicalism in the past century, and it has proven to be insufficient in making disciples.

Jesus came preaching the kingdom of God, not as a future "escape" clause but as a challenge to live out God's purposes for life in the present. Anabaptists grasped the Sermon on the Mount as a manifesto given for just such a purpose. When Jesus sent out the seventy-two "other disciples," he told them to go out and heal people saying, "The kingdom of God has come near to you" (Luke 10:9). And when the Pharisees asked about the coming of the kingdom of God, Jesus answered them saying that the kingdom will not come as they expect; rather, "The kingdom of God is in the midst of you," or as other translations put it, "within you" (Luke 17:20-22). Those who make decisions must be taught that they are not escaping this world through faith in Christ but are sent back into the world to reveal the kingdom of God and its transforming power. That power makes a person different in business, in relationship, and in every conceivable way.

One further critique of "The Decision" underscores the pressure to evangelize and extract the decision to believe in Christ from a prospective believer. It seems the pressure rests primarily on the decision, but not on what happens afterward. Discipleship, walking alongside a new believer, was not a primary consideration and thus not taught as part of aggressive evangelism. A man in his late sixties once shared his teenage experience of being wooed by other youths in a local church. They befriended him and included him in many of their activities, making him feel special when he came to church. Progressing in his faith, he was encouraged to receive baptism and join the church membership. Once the young man was "in," those who had befriended him suddenly disappeared, relationally speaking, and did not have time for him anymore. When later the young man slipped into old "sinful" habits, the church asked him to leave because he was not upholding the lifestyle of the community. If "The Decision" does not lead to discipleship, more embittered converts will revert to the friendship circles that were more accepting and encouraging. It is no cliché to say that people often feel more welcome in a bar than in the church.

---

39 Mark 10:17-22

The Danger of "Jesus and Me"

Decision-driven evangelism makes faith a solitary affair between the individual and God. Individualism has made faith a private affair so that what the individual believes about God is nobody's business but their own. "Each to his own," and "You are free to believe what you believe. Just don't ask me to believe it too," are the common refrains regarding faith. The North American mindset that individual faith is a private matter does not make the individual publicly accountable. What one thinks or feels about God and Jesus is between "me and my conscience." Faith is anything you want it to be under these conditions.

Here evangelicalism might be applauded for persisting in evangelizing the lost and not allowing a person to be left alone. Yet, once the evangelical has "saved" a lost soul, what does she do with him? Rodney Clapp quotes Harold Bloom who said, "Salvation for the American cannot come through the community or congregation, but is a one-on-one act of confrontation with God."[40] The individual comes to God alone through a personal subjective experience where God revealed himself in a dramatic or palpable manner, or so the individual is led to believe. Individualism of this sort has been at play since the eighteenth century; reversing its effects will not be a simple task.

Our worship experience perpetuates the individual nature of faith, specifically in the songs we sing. Many of our worship songs in the assembly of believers emphasize individualism. Popular "praise and worship" songs more suited for the radio than for corporate worship speak of "I" and "me" in response to the wonders of God. One example contains the lyrics, "Like a rose trampled on the ground you took the fall and thought of me above all."[41] Wiser scholars have argued that the lyrics can be taken in context to affirm that Jesus died "for me," so judgment will be reserved on this aspect. The issue being underscored here is that corporate worship often sings "me" instead of "we" as the body comes *together* to worship God. Where do evangelicals teach the "we" of being the body of Christ? Even American hymnody provides evidence that individualism has tainted it with lyrics where Jesus "walks with me and talks with me."

Wes Michaelson reflected on the contra-communal nature of individualistic worship when he wrote:

> Because evangelical spirituality has been so highly individualistic, there usually has been little experience of the church as a community. What communal sense there is has resulted more from a legalistic

---

40   Rodney Clapp, *A Peculiar People* (Downers Grove, IL: InterVarsity Press, 1996), 34.
41   Michael W. Smith sang "Above All," written by Lenny Leblanc and Paul Beloche. Capitol Christian Music Group, Universal Music Publishing Group, 2001.

separation from the outside world than the reality of koinonia as it is described in the New Testament. Most evangelical worship has been designed to bolster personal piety rather than to nurture the corporate life of Christ's body.[42]

N.T. Wright notes that once we grasp this individualism, the "pro me of the gospel, the idea that God is 'being gracious to me,' we no longer need to be too firmly rooted in history." Individualism cringes at a historical Jesus, for a historical Jesus might reveal a particular God with a character and purpose different from one's own personalized perception of God. And if Jesus calls the believer into community, one's own agenda may be circumvented by the will of the community. Submitting to the will of the community of Christ, the church, runs against the North American mindset of discovering and relating to God by one's self.[43]

c) The Christian Nation: The myth of the Christian nation applies to the belief that because the majority religion is Christian and can influence policy at a federal level, they identify as a Christian nation. Perhaps that definition belies a simplistic understanding. One nation more than any other fits that definition in the current context—the United States.

G. K. Chesterton once said that America is a nation with the soul of a church. Evangelicals would delight in this characterization, and through some special hermeneutics, consider this prophetic. The flip side of Chesterton's observation reveals another side of US self-awareness: "The US church is the church with a soul of a nation." Clapp comments,

Because we have so readily privatized faith, we find that the institutional or corporate expression of our faith can occur only through the indisputably political entity called the United States of America. In a way, then, this is another aspect of Gnosticizing the Christian church.[44]

The recent 2016 presidential election highlighted the power of the evangelical church in the US to elect a candidate. Given the options before them, evangelicals exerted their influence on voters holding up one candidate as the only option while citing the opponent as "bad news" for America. Both options were questionable from a moral point of view. However, much grace was shown to the "evangelically approved" candidate since it was well known that the person in question was a womanizer and a ruthless businessman.

---

42 Kraus, *Evangelicalism and Anabaptism*, Ch. 4 "Evangelicalism and Radical Discipleship" by Wes Michaelson, 65.
43 Clapp, *Peculiar People*, 35.
44 Clapp, *Peculiar People*, 45.

When the "religious right" or "moral majority" put their support behind the preferred candidate, evangelicals were set on who they were to vote for in the coming election. They were by no means blind to the imperfections of the candidate but were spurred on by the positive results that went far beyond the four-year term.[45]

Evangelicals are unapologetic concerning their involvement in national politics and are self-aware in terms of their objectives under the guise of being a Christian nation. Timothy Paul Erdel has identified five arguments regarding evangelical participation in US politics:

1. The United States is a Christian nation, one exceptional in its mission and calling.
2. Christians should actively seek to establish and enforce Christian values within our Christian nation.[46]
3. The electoral process is the appropriate means to accomplish such a goal, given that electing the right government officeholders will more likely result in the appropriate political legislation, executive orders, and judicial appointments, since the latter will also more likely lead to correct interpretations of the United States constitution, of the laws enacted by right-minded legislators, and of properly motivated executive orders.
4. Further loss of biblical values in our nation may be directly attributed to the loss of an election by the Republican party, which is clearly the only viable political party (at least at this time) in terms of enacting and supporting Christian values.
5. Thus, the rapid loss of Christian values that would all but inevitably follow from a Democratic party victory at the polls would in turn soon bring about the end of this present age.[47]

Putting one's faith in Christ means more than simply being saved from one's sins and living one's own life. When a person receives Christ as Lord, that person's whole life will be transformed by the mind of Christ. That person will see the world differently and will engage the world's evils as a representative of Christ. Evangelicals take that belief to heart. Historically, evan-

---

45　Many evangelicals noted that a Republican president would appoint a favorable person for the vacant position of Supreme Court justice. Since there are no terms for justices, this person would serve long after the president completed his term in office. American friends shared that a pro-life Supreme Court justice was the hoped-for result.
46　Jared S. Burkholder, ed. *The Activist Impulse* (Eugene, OR: Pickwick Publications, 2012), Ch. 12 "Go Tell That Fox," Timothy Paul Erdel, 328.
47　Ibid, 329.

gelicals have been actively involved in addressing social ills. Not only were they to build the fellowship of the church, but they believed they were also to make war on sin wherever it was found.

In England, the evangelical fervor that drove Christians to engage social injustices through politics laid hold of William Wilberforce (1759-1833). His evangelical convictions regarding slavery and the slave trade propelled him to lobby the government to abolish slavery. Wilberforce said,

> So enormous, so dreadful, so irremediable did the [slave] trade's wickedness appear that my own mind was completely made up for abolition. Let the consequences be what they would: I from this time determined that I would never rest until I had effected its abolition.

Others of the evangelical mindset joined him in this crusade and won the campaign just three days before Wilberforce died.

In pre-Civil War America, evangelicals were also leaders in social reform. Their conviction, like Wilberforce's, was that Christian engagement with life and culture meant more than winning souls for Christ, it also meant transforming life and culture through a gospel-inspired influence. Evangelicals turned their attention to working conditions, voting rights for women, prison reform, humane treatment for the mentally ill, the temperance movement, and of course—the abolition of slavery. After the Civil War, a shift occurred—evangelicals were not as socially active. By the 1920s, evangelicals began to separate personal salvation from social salvation.

Many of the goals mentioned above were not realized immediately, but in time, slavery was abolished and, much later, women did get the vote. Behind the movement to transform society was the belief that God was working in the United States as his chosen nation. Evangelicals truly believed they were the new Israel, God's chosen people, and some still do today. Politically and theologically, the American people believed they had a "manifest destiny" to usher in the kingdom of God. They saw themselves as a "city on a hill" that could not be hidden, but that would be a shining example to the rest of the world of what a Christian nation would look like with a proper government under God.[48] That destiny would lead America to make decisions in the global community that would enforce their example upon nations for their betterment.

---

48 Matthew 5:14 – "You are the light of the world. A city set on a hill cannot be hidden." American evangelicals took this verse personally to mean that they as a nation were a model of godly government for all the world to see.

The Problem of the Christian Nation

In an ideal context, the vision of a Christian nation where politicians made decisions by praying in Congress and in the Senate and seeking the wisdom of God through careful study of the Bible would be a marvelous thing. If all courts would seek justice and reconciliation between parties, uphold the life of the unborn, mediate between couples seeking a divorce, and work at reforming criminals instead of locking them away, society would be transformed in unheard-of ways. If America were a Christian nation, the issue of race and discrimination would be a thing of the past.

But not every politician is Christian. Not all Americans place their trust and faith in Christ. Not all Americans share the values of evangelicalism. And so there is a conflict in America: Christian values stand in opposition to the whole of America, and vice versa. The evangelical Christian response to this conflict is to gain political office and impress their values on a nation of diverse beliefs and values. Evangelicals are, after all, right.

The following is true of every nation that misguidedly believes they are a Christian nation. America simply stands out as the greater example of how the myth of being a Christian nation plays out.

First, the ideology of a "Christian nation" reveals unbelief in the influence of the church upon the world. If evangelical Christians believe social justice and transformation comes only through political power, then, conversely, the church has no part to play in and of itself in the redemption of society. Evangelicals have not tapped into their God-given imaginations and the gifts of the Holy Spirit if they believe they have to hold political office or sway the elective process to bring healing to the nation. The would-be evangelical politician is woefully deluded if he or she believes they can make a difference in government without making compromises and shipwrecking their faith in Christ in the process. In Canada, as is surely true of American politics, a Member of Parliament or a Member of the Legislature does not vote upon their convictions, but upon the party platform they represent.

Second, the ideology of a "Christian nation" organizes Christians to do the work of Christ apart from the church. Again, the church in North America as a venue for social change begs to be activated to its full potential. Blocking this potential is the persistent argument that the church provides only spiritual and social comforts, while real-world change happens only in the political arena. From civic to federal politics, well-meaning Christians involve themselves in policymaking instead of developing a vision for the church to engage society in a meaningful, practical way.

Third, belief in a "Christian nation" views the effectiveness of the church as solely an evangelism agency. Social justice issues, evangelicals believe, are best addressed by political agencies. Evangelical churches in Canada were involved in caring for the poor and homeless until the Canadian Welfare movement was enacted in the 1960s. Other government agencies were established to address social needs, and the church backed off. Credit must be given to the government for creating social programs; the tragedy was that the imagination of the church stagnated. Instead of coming alongside the government agencies or addressing new concerns, the church focused on spiritual concerns alone.

Fourth, evangelicals believe that the "Christian nation" persists through voting. "Real Change" offered by politicians deludes the populace into voting yet again to transform the nation into something good. Time and again, voters are disappointed by the failure of the elected to bring about the changes they had promised. Yet they vote again because this time it will be different. Influencing the nation, the city, or the neighborhood for Christ cannot be done through political manipulation. And if the evangelical voters succeed in "winning" and placing their candidate in office, morality cannot be legislated. Erdel asks a timely question: Should Christian values guide secular society? [49]

Fifth, there is no such thing as a Christian nation. In the book of Daniel, the reader will observe the clash of faith in the living God with the idolatry of a pagan nation. When Daniel prays despite an edict forbidding prayer, public or private, except to king Darius, he falls afoul of the "government." Evangelicals like to cite this incident in view of the lack of prayer in public schools and would love to see prayer legislated back into schools. America is a Christian nation, they say, and prayer should be allowed in all arenas of life. Commenting on Daniel 6, Tremper Longman III had this to say:

> The confusion in the United States and probably other Western democracies arises because some Christians insist that their country is the modern equivalent of Israel. However, it cannot be urged too strongly that there are and can be no modern equivalents of Israel. There is no such thing as a "Christian nation," except in the sense of a nation where most of the inhabitants happen to be Christian at that particular historical moment.[50]

---

[49] See Timothy Paul Erdel's chapter "Go Tell That Fox" in *The Activist Impulse* for an insightful response to this question, 330 ff.

[50] Tremper Longman III, *Daniel: The NIV Application Commentary* (Grand Rapids, MI: Zondervan, 1999), 170.

After Christ introduced the new covenant in the Gospels, no nation can be said to be "the chosen people" since the kingdom of God spreads across borders and racial divides. To put it another way, the kingdom of God cannot be contained by the artificial boundaries of policy and border.

The evangelical church must operate with this in mind. To influence public policy for social justice parallels the call of Christ to be salt and light, but to try to legislate morality for those who neither know Christ nor believe in him does not advance the kingdom—it makes evangelicals into bullies. Evangelicals need to exorcise Chesterton's evaluation and become the church with the soul of a church. Constantinianism must not be allowed to water down the church again. Longman responds in a radical and, one might surmise, unpopular way, writing:

> In other words, that nation is not the church. The modern equivalent of Israel is not a political entity but rather the church. Christians should be working to keep prayer out of public schools, manger scenes off the front yard of city hall, and the Ten Commandments out of the local magistrates' offices. When the church has state backing, it grows complacent, or even worse, coercive in its witness. Indeed, study has shown that when the church gets an entrée into the power structures of the state (whether the government per se or public educational institutions), it has hurt, not helped, the cause of the kingdom.[51]

Longman speaks prophetically that the church cannot be the church when it clothes itself with the emperor's clothes. The experiment under Constantine failed and the church ought never to align itself again with the state.

In Canada, evangelicals are under less of an illusion than our American brothers and sisters. Yet Canadian evangelicals do at times fall under a peculiar spell of self-deception. In the middle of the twentieth century, it was said that per capita, Canada was more evangelical than the United States. Over the last few decades, there was a sharp decline, and today, Canada bears no resemblance to that past image. The spell persists.

Speaking to an assembled group of university students, professors, and scholars at Providence University College, John Stackhouse Jr. put a pin in the bubble of evangelical self-deception in Canada. An excerpt from his talk reveals the mirage under which Canadian Christians dwell. The piece is called "If Canada were a Christian nation":

---

51 Longman III, 170.

What if Canada were still strongly Christian, how would we behave?
We would attend church, but maybe just once a week.
We would maintain social relationships, receive reinforcement for our beliefs and values, and enjoy worship.

There would be no strong pressure to conform to non-Christian patterns. Everything around us would be reinforcing Christian values.

We would read the Bible and pray, but just sometimes.
Mostly to deal with crises.
There would be no concern that every day poses serious challenges and include formative experiences for which we need guidance from God's Word. Thus, we would not need to read God's Word all that often.

We would tithe, but just a small amount.
Because plenty of other people can give. Many people richer than I am who can give. I am already contributing to the public welfare through my taxes.
There are lots of volunteers so little need for paid staff.

I would volunteer, but not very much.
Because plenty of other people can volunteer. There's lots of volunteers so I do not need to volunteer that much.

We would learn, but only the basics, and in fun easy modes in entertaining ways.
There are no serious intellectual challenges.
There are no serious ethical quandaries.
What I don't know, others do.
So I would attend the occasional Bible or book study group and read the occasional web article.

I would converse with Christians. But not about serious matters.
There are no serious intellectual challenges. I could talk about hockey or real estate.
There are no serious ethical quandaries; everyone sees things the same way.
Everyone has plenty of spiritual and moral support

I would desire to be ethical, but without any discipline.

> Everyone is basically good, so no need for regular and searching introspection.
> No need for regimes of accountability. Everyone's going to do the right thing anyways.
>
> We would want to share the gospel, but only with family.
> NO one holds a significantly different worldview.
> Everyone already knows the gospel.
>
> I would have a concern for public life, but without worries.
> Only Christian elites dominate public discourse.
> Only Christian forces shape society.
> There would be no need for strategic preparation of Christians to enter and improve public life; it's already so Christian.
>
> We would support Christian education, but just in churches.
> Private and homeschooling would be needlessly expensive.
> Public schools teach the same values.
> Christian higher education would be redundant.
>
> Canada today is not Christian, but we are acting as if it is. I've described the way Canadian Christians act today.[52]

Canadian evangelicals live in a dreamworld at times and are outraged at the decline of morality in Canada and, like their American counterparts, seek change through voting in political candidates who best represent their values. Statistics reveal, however, that only 10 percent of Canadians identify as evangelical.[53] They do not hold the same sway the American evangelical possesses in voting, and party leaders do not cater to them by claiming to be "born again." Consequently, Canadian evangelicals have significantly less influence on Canadian politics than American evangelicals.

In summary, no matter the nation at issue, there can never be a Christian nation so long as imperfect, ambitious men and women vie for power in the halls of government. Living in the false security of this myth only serves to make Christians lazy in their interaction with society. If evangelicals want to make a difference for Christ, they will need to wake up to the reality that

---

52 Dr. John Stackhouse Jr. "The Reformation Then and Now" (Part 2) Given at Providence University College in Otterburne, MB, October 31, 2017. Stackhouse serves as Professor of Religious Studies & Dean of Faculty Development at Crandall University in Moncton, NB.
53 "Religious Affiliation and Attendance in Canada." Accessed March 12, 2019. http://www.in-trust.org/Magazine/Issues/New-Year-2016/Religious-affiliation-and-attendance-in-Canada.

they are living in enemy territory, the kingdom ruled by the prince of the power of the air.[54] Expectations will change, as evangelicals will realize that not everyone in school prays, that morality cannot be legislated, and that one's neighbor does not go to church. When grieving this false impression concludes, evangelicals can begin to see the opportunities to share Christ in a fallen world with broken people.

d) "The Plan": In concert with "the decision" and the aggressive evangelistic push to sell Christianity is the bonus offer: the plan. Individuals lost in a world of meaninglessness and looking for a sense of purpose are naturally drawn to the promise of divine purpose. The "witness" shares with the "lost soul" that God has a wonderful plan for his or her life. Taken literally and personally, the convert takes this to mean that from now on, everything will be laid out before him or her by a caring God: whom they will marry; what job they will receive; success in no uncertain terms in every sphere of life.

When evangelicals repeat this oft-used term, "the plan," are they correct in their offers to the convert? Does God promise to intricately direct our steps so that every decision will be clear for the individual? Speakers like Joel Osteen would have his listeners believe that "success" is the greatest mark of the Christian. American evangelicals believe "the plan" includes "life, liberty, and the pursuit of happiness," as stated in their Declaration of Independence. Yet for many, happiness is elusive even as they follow Christ.

The comfort of "the plan" to the average follower of Christ is that everything happens for a reason. Everything that happens to an evangelical will turn out for God's glory. Even death. Try telling that to a prospective mother who miscarries her child. How is this God's plan, she will ask? Can the evangelical confidently look at tragedy and smilingly declare that "God's got this" while people grieve over crushed hopes and dreams? Would the Christ of the Gospels wave off their weeping and tell them, "It's all part of the plan?"

Evangelicals themselves are wrestling with disillusionment over the misunderstanding of "the plan." They, too, are wondering what preachers mean by God's purposes when everything falls apart. When the plan does not unfold like the Osteens promise it will, the individual must lack faith.

As the characters on the TV sitcom "Modern Family" often ask, "What's the plan, Phil?" we too must ask: What's the plan? For there is a plan; it just might not be what the "Four Spiritual Laws" implied.

A favorite biblical reference for the proponents of "the plan" is Proverbs 3:5-6: "Trust in the LORD with all your heart, and do not lean on your own

---

54 Ephesians 2:2

understanding. In all your ways acknowledge him, and he will make straight your paths." Every word of this verse is true. How evangelicals understand the verse reveals a problem. One common misunderstanding of the verse suggests that any difficulties, all obstacles in one's path, and the trials of life will suddenly disappear. However, God does not promise a carefree life once a person puts their trust in Jesus; he does promise to make one's path straight. The life of Christ, whom believers are to follow in imitation, died on a cross after having been beaten and scourged. Most of the disciples, save for John, lost their lives in martyrdom. Paul suffered as an apostle, not only at the hands of unbelieving Jews but also as a target for divided churches. Jesus told his followers that they should not be surprised that the world hates them because the world hated him first.

In a world of pain and loss, North American evangelicalism lacks a theology of suffering. When "the plan" is offered to potential converts as a cure to all their problems, they are deceived by the mirage of happiness and eventually disillusioned with the faith when happiness proves elusive. Jesus and his apostles never taught the crowds that life would get easier when they put their faith in him. In fact, he said to all who were following him, "If anyone would come after me, let him deny himself and take up his cross daily and follow me. For whoever would save his life will lose it, but whoever loses his life for my sake will save it" (Luke 9:23-24).

Returning to the Proverbs text, the promise that paths will be straightened demands proper context. God has given every person the opportunity to chart a course for his or her life, to pursue a career or lifestyle, and to marry whom they want, within the parameters of his will. That statement offers a broad scope of options. Within that scope, the one who puts his or her trust in God must acknowledge that God's "royal law," to love God and love your neighbor, governs how we operate in those different dimensions of life. When one does this, whatever the circumstances, God will "straighten" the path, he will make it clear *how* one operates in faithful obeisance.

In critiquing "the plan," the reader must understand that what is proposed here does not negate the "grand plan" of God. God's grand plan involves bringing all of history to a final and victorious conclusion for Christ and those who follow him by bringing to fruition the kingdom of God in its entirety upon the earth. Even the seeking of God's guidance for specific issues and trials need not be discouraged by this proposal.

Evangelicals need to be careful is in their presumption upon God's promises that present and material success means "blessing." Jesus taught enough about the dangers of wealth and power that evangelicals who love the Bible ought not to be led down that "prosperity" path. God has a plan; God is at work in the life of believers; God grants wisdom to those who ask for it (James 1:5).

Evangelical attitudes toward God's deliverance need to be more like Shadrach, Meshach, and Abednego, who declared "Our God will deliver us, but if he does not…" (Daniel 3:17-18). Or as the apostle Paul wrote, "Indeed, we felt that we had received the sentence of death. But that was to make us rely not on ourselves but on God who raises the dead," (2 Corinthians 1:9). Both instances strongly suggest that our plans (ambitions, hopes, dreams) and God's plans do not always line up, but we can trust God that his grand plan will not disappoint us.

Conclusion

Modern evangelicalism has given the church a fervor for evangelizing the individual and offering personal salvation. When one accepts Jesus Christ, the assurance of salvation is confirmed through the presence of the Holy Spirit and subsequent works based on grace. These elements of evangelical faith cannot be understated. If individualism has been overemphasized, the corrective will be found in the renewal of the importance of the faith community. Individualism has counteracted the impersonal and brought God near. However, the evangelical message needs to be adjusted to remind the one that faith in Christ brings the one into the many. With the many comes accountability and the rejection of "private" faith. Following Christ in life makes the disciple stand out so that there can be no privacy to faith.

Where evangelicalism has disappointed and disillusioned many in the church, syncretism and culture are to blame for the most part. Evangelicals have allowed the culture to choose the tune they dance to instead of dancing a countercultural jig. Trying to fit into the mainstream of Western thinking and acting has watered down the contrast that should exist between the world and the church. Attempting to use a political office as a medium to transform culture has failed and created unnecessary enemies among the populace. If the world hates you, it should not be for manipulating an election.

Evangelicalism need not be rejected by the church. A reformation that reclaims the evangelical fervor of seeking the lost sheep and transforming culture through social justice and serving "the least of these" would definitely recover the reputation of the movement among Christians. This book proposes that evangelicalism may once again be the hands and feet of Christ in the world through syncing with Anabaptist perspectives of the gospel of Jesus Christ. The two can complement one another, as has been evident in the merging streams presented in these chapters. Various doctrinal and social tensions need to be hammered out, but the prognosis for evangelicalism is hopeful. Evangelical culture may have failed, but evangelical theology is still needed, together with Anabaptist ethics.

For those who want to "break up" with evangelicalism and who just want to be followers of Christ, these evangelical truths still have value. We do not need more labels, but we do need to redefine what it means to be evangelical in the twenty-first century.

Chapter Three:
How We Read the Bible

Reading the Bible should not be thought of as the work of scholars alone. Ever since Gutenberg invented his printing press and Wycliffe, Tyndale, Luther, and others worked to put the Bible into the hands of the common person, the impact of reading the Bible has transformed countless lives. Far be it from scholars to take this revelation of God away from the non-academic and make it unreachable.

Faithful readers of the Bible must admit, however, that some difficult texts in the Bible require more than a cursory glance. Yes, we can easily interpret and apply John 3:16, and we readily know what it means to "love your neighbor," but the average reader will stumble over the meaning of "the end of the age" in Mark 13. Biblical scholars have done a great service in combing through the ancient languages and cultures to present the modern reader with tools to understand the meanings beneath the text. Hermeneutics may be called the science of studying the Bible, and evangelicals have provided us with a wealth of writers and thinkers to help the student of the Bible elucidate the text.

Evangelicals and Anabaptists agree on the starting point for knowing God and discovering his will for living in his creation—the Bible. Both share a high view of Scripture, affirming the foundation it presents for faith in Christ. They may differ in how they arrive at understanding and applying the truths of the Bible. If a conflict exists between the two streams of Christian perspective regarding the Bible, the chasm does not need to be great. Anabaptists rely upon evangelical scholarship to interpret and proclaim the message of the Scriptures, and many Anabaptist writers contribute to the great library of tools. In the next generation, the two movements can take advantage of a cooperative approach to evangelical and Anabaptist methods of reading, studying, and applying the truths of Scripture.

Beginning with evangelical hermeneutics, we will explore the process of interpreting Scripture. The reader will then be introduced to the Anabaptist methodology of community hermeneutics. Our goal will be extracting the best of both methods to establish a foundation for an evangelical-Anabaptist hybrid.

How Evangelicals Read the Bible

Evangelical hermeneutics have informed many readers of the Bible so that the lens of interpretation might be sound. People of all walks of life may pick up the Bible and read; they can read and be led to salvation through believing in Jesus Christ, and by reading they can know how they should live in a Christlike manner. Many will affirm the simplicity of the above statements and scorn the need for a further exegesis of the texts, saying that scholarship just complicates the process. However, one need only examine history and find that many have been led astray by those who misused the texts of Scripture for their own gain, or out of ignorance assumed that they knew best. Sound hermeneutics are essential to keeping the body of Christ from error and apostasy.

Richard Longenecker wrote on the task of hermeneutics, saying:

> Hermeneutics—the theory, method and practice of how to read, understand, and use biblical texts—is at the heart of Christian identity, has profound effects on the formulation of Christian theology, informs every aspect of Christian living, and gives guidance to the church's proclamation and mission. It is, in fact, foundational for every reading of Scripture, every expression of Christian conviction, and all Christian living, whether personal or corporate.[55]

Longenecker, in the same paper, presents three tasks of doing hermeneutics. What follows is a brief summary of the three tasks, which are by no means representative of the extent of the work of interpretation.

The evangelical hermeneutic begins with what Longenecker calls the Interpretive/Descriptive Task. Having observed the text and noted words, phrases, and repetitions, the next step involves understanding those words, thoughts, and authorial intentions in their given contexts. Everyone who interprets the Bible will take this step.

Where evangelicals differ with other traditions is found in their assumptions regarding the Bible. Longenecker emphasizes that Christian thought and life begins with the assumption that God has revealed himself in the experience of the nation of Israel in the Old Testament, and then uniquely through the person and work of Jesus Christ of Nazareth. These revelations were interpreted by the apostles who were witnesses of Jesus, the fulfillment of the prophecies, and taught as truth to the early church. These truths were illuminated and

---

[55] Richard N. Longenecker, "Major Tasks of an Evangelical Hermeneutic: Some Observations on Commonalities Interrelations, and Differences" *Bulletin for Biblical Research* 14.1 (2004) 45-58. Longenecker is a professor at Wycliffe College, University of Toronto.

applied by the Holy Spirit. Thus, the Christian faith is a religion of revelation: the good news of God prophesied through Israel's prophets, fulfilled in Jesus, witnessed by the apostles, and verified by the Holy Spirit in the church.

This revelation came to the prophets and apostles through various historical settings and methods. The Bible was written over fifteen hundred years by men and women who received visions and dreams, who heard the voice of God, who were inspired by the Spirit to write poetry, history, and prose. They came from different cultures and contexts and wrote in Hebrew, Greek, and Aramaic. God used writers who persisted under the pressures and influences of foreign powers, including Assyria, Babylon, Persia, Greece, and Rome. So, in seeking to understand the words, thoughts, and intentions of these writers, the reader must investigate the specific situations, the cultural concerns, and the rules of writing and thinking in those days. When the writer of Daniel speaks of beasts coming out of the sea, the reader would be aided in knowing that Babylonian creation myths play a significant role in the imagery and purpose of what Daniel witnessed.

The key to proper biblical interpretation is the attention given first to the author's intent in writing. Most modern Bible readers want to jump to the application before stopping to consider what the author was trying to say to the people in his time, in the midst of an idolatrous culture and from the mindset of a first-century person living the ancient near east. Akin to this attitude toward the text is the attempt to grasp the biblical writer's interpretation of Scripture: How did the first-century believer understand prophecy in relation to the Messiah Jesus? The modern reader is tempted to read back into the text a twenty-first century, modern, Western interpretation, and remembering to seek authorial intent will prevent poor interpretation habits. A proper exegesis will keep the lens of interpretation centered on the author's mind, so far as this is possible.

The second task of an evangelical Hermeneutic is the Transformational Task, otherwise known as the application of the biblical message to daily life. This step of interpretation takes the message of the biblical writers and considers what would be the outworking of this message in conduct and thought. With the direction of the Holy Spirit, the evangelical will take the writer's intention and make it operative in the Christian life as normative in the gospel proclamation. Longenecker concedes that what different groups of evangelicals consider normative may differ considerably. At stake in both tasks is the concern for the essence of the biblical message and what it means for Christ-followers today.

Longenecker confesses that the difference between the two tasks, the Interpretive and the Transformational, is that the former is based on research and reflection, while the latter demands a personal response of faith and a commitment to living out these principles. One does not live out these principles in isolation as a "lone ranger" Christian; we learn these truths and applications through the church where faith is lived and understood. Christ's life, work, and teaching, having been revealed in the context of the Gospels, must be the primary focus of the Transformational Task. And the evangelical must not forget that the ministry of the Holy Spirit makes possible the actual expression of Christ's life, work, and teaching in the life of the church.

Finally, the third task of evangelical Hermeneutics is the Contextualization Task. Longenecker writes that this task involves "the expression of the Christian gospel in the various cultural contexts and specific situations of today." The student of the Bible takes the message the first two tasks have revealed and attempts to put it into the context of the person or people groups one wants to address. Missionaries specifically are challenged with understanding the culture of the people groups so they may appropriately share the good news of Christ in a manner that resonates with that people group. In a transient world where people are moving out of their countries of origin and moving abroad, missionaries are not the only ones who need to consider an unfamiliar culture when sharing Christ. How does the evangelical gospeler effectively communicate the message of the risen Christ to the immigrant family down the street?

There are many challenges when opening the Bible to people who have never seen one before. Those new to the Bible may wonder why there are four gospels when we speak of "the" gospel. And why are there discrepancies in the testimony of the four writers? Why did Paul, the apostle to the Gentiles, write so many letters to different churches when he only had one message? Details that evangelicals who have grown up with the Bible take for granted must be dealt with if the message of the good news will be communicated with the uninitiated.

The process of interpreting the Scriptures, particularly the New Testament, involves these three tasks. Neither of these tasks can be circumvented if we are to properly understand the gospel message and apply that message to life and thought. The first task involves discovering the original message as the author intended to convey it and understanding what it means for personal and corporate living; the second task expresses in real terms the first task; and the third task of evangelical hermeneutics considers what those expressions might look like in the context of various cultures.

Whether the student of the Bible engages these three tasks or follows the similar inductive method, there are rules for studying and interpreting the Bible.[56] Objectors may naively counter that they do not need rules; they can

---

56 Inductive Bible Study uses the three phases of Observation-Interpretation-Application to unpack a text of Scripture.

simply read and understand the Bible in its current form. Current studies in literature believe otherwise since even reading Shakespeare requires a set of rules to grasp his meaning. The contribution of evangelical hermeneutics rests squarely on this point, that we have come to understand the Bible more sufficiently because of these rules.

How Anabaptists Read the Bible

Mennonite historian John Roth said that the Anabaptists originally approached hermeneutics without a set of rules.[57] They believed the interpretation of Scripture was straightforward and did not need to be complicated with various filters. Given that sixteenth-century Anabaptists were outlaws in most states and were on the run from authorities, they did not have the time or luxury of studying the Bible. This simple approach to Scripture continued even after the persecution of the movement subsided. One might propose that the average twenty-first-century Anabaptist carries on this simple approach to hermeneutics, but that would be unfair to the many Anabaptist college and seminary students who have begun to populate the church.

The poor practice of hermeneutics has proven disastrous in the history of Anabaptism. The Muenster Tragedy, where early Anabaptists took over the city of Muenster believing that the New Jerusalem would be established there was based on a faulty interpretation of eschatological texts. Then there was the Peasants Revolt, another slaughter of the naïve and uninformed. Another incident that occurred due to a poor hermeneutic was the case where grown adults played with toys and babbled like babies because Jesus said that one must become like a little child to enter the kingdom of God. And in the early nineteenth century, an Anabaptist sect was involved in a "humility movement," which demanded that its adherents weep in prayer before partaking in supper. Some would lay in ditches to show their humble posture before God and community. These are just a few examples of misguided expressions of piety based on a shallow hermeneutic in Anabaptist circles.

Eventually, the Anabaptists began to develop a set of principles for interpreting Scriptures. For most of the Anabaptist movement's existence, no theological institutions were dedicated to their method of study. At the very least, this hermeneutic was developed in community, as will be evident in the following explanations.

How did Anabaptists approach the Bible?

---

57   John Roth, *Beliefs: Mennonite Faith and Practice*. (Scottdale, PA: Herald Press, 2005), 43.

First, the Anabaptists believe the Bible speaks authoritatively to the Christian life. The devout follower of Christ will find that the Bible is the source for understanding the essence of faith and how that faith may be expressed in life. If the church stagnates because of internal and external influences, church renewal will only be achieved through Scripture alone. If the church flourishes, it will be because that community of faith continues to find its nourishment and nurture in the Word of God. For this reason, the Anabaptist movement involved a consistent and regular gathering of the faithful for Bible study. In these times of study, Anabaptists found that all theological questions would be answered through searching the Scriptures.[58]

Since the gathering of Anabaptists for Bible study was a core feature of their life together, they believed no individual could interpret Scripture in isolation; interpretation could only be properly accomplished in community. Everyone comes to the text of Scripture in various ways, from different cultural backgrounds and with different faith traditions. Any person with a computer has access to a wide array of information sources, including biblical interpretations, so no one can claim to come to Bible interpretation without preconceptions. Anabaptists believe that, since individual interpretation can be so broad, the Bible should be read as a congregation, as opposed to listening only to experts. Scholars, pastors, commentators, and the like thus have no final say on the interpretation of a text. If churches leave interpretation up to the colleges and seminaries, the community of faith surrenders their responsibility to discern the faith of the life of the body of believers. Certainly, resources like commentaries and Bible dictionaries are welcome, but these sources are not the final authority in interpretation.[59]

In response to the community approach of the Anabaptists to reading and interpreting the Bible, the evangelical hermeneutic may appear as a contrast to some degree. Douglas Groothuis wrote:

> Given the postmodernist critique of language, some are claiming that an emphasis on the Bible as propositional revelation is problematic or even errant. They argue that our view of Scripture must be re-evaluated. Community should take precedent over doctrinal positions…along these lines, some claim that theology should be primarily narratival in nature and not systematic or abstract. Telling the Christian story should replace stipulating Christian doctrine.[60]

58　Ibid, 43.
59　Stuart Murray in a presentation at **Be in Christ Church of Canada**, Session Two – "How Anabaptists Read the Bible." June 10, 2014, The Meeting House, Oakville, ON.
60　Douglas Groothuis, *Themelios* "The Postmodernist Challenge to Theology." vol. 25 no. 1 Nov. 1999, p. 4.

Groothuis was writing in response to postmodernist challenges to theology, but he could have just as easily have been critiquing the Anabaptist community hermeneutic.

Jerome (347-420) may have said, "The Scriptures are shallow enough for a babe to come and drink without fear of drowning and deep enough for a theologian to swim in without ever touching the bottom." Though Augustine, Bishop of Hippo (354-430) said something similar, "The Bible is shallow enough for a child not to drown, yet deep enough for an elephant to swim." Oddly enough, Jerome translated the Bible into Latin, thereby making the Bible inaccessible for centuries to the common reader since few but the scholarly could read Latin. Nevertheless, both men are correct in their comments concerning the Bible. Anabaptists rightly deduced that the Bible belonged to everyone and everyone should have access to it. If ordinary people wrote the Bible, then ordinary people should be able to read it and understand it. Consequently, to rely on one voice, even the pastor's, to interpret Scripture for the congregation implies that the Bible is out of their grasp and demeans the average congregant as incapable of understanding the Bible.

Those who come to Scripture will not leave empty-handed. Anabaptists believed the Holy Spirit was at work in the preaching, teaching, and sharing of the Scriptures so that if a person was open to the leading of the Spirit and the collective wisdom of the congregation, they ought not to leave the gathering without a morsel of truth to gnaw upon. The Holy Spirit actively engages the group, guiding the reading and reflection, helping the participants to make connections between text and text and text and life, and bringing to mind how these truths work out in the real world.[61]

What of the individual? With this corporate emphasis on interpretation, would there be a place for personal study of the Bible and prayer? Anabaptists surely encouraged a personal reading of the Bible, and at the present time, even more so, but they understood that the work of interpretation should be done in the church. No individual had the corner on interpretation.

A word of caution is necessary regarding the collective hermeneutic of Anabaptist practice. The principle of a community hermeneutic guards against the individualism of our generation and puts the responsibility for interpretation back on the church. However, well-meaning congregations have at times agreed on a set course of action based on what they believed was a biblical mandate only to discover later that they were wrong. An individual committed to the truth of Scripture and guided by the Holy Spirit may need to speak out prophetically against the wrong actions of a group if they collectively decide to

---

61 Murray.

err. Becoming culturally relevant or caving to the cultural norms are real temptations in this age and will certainly color the interpretation of Scripture if a congregation does not heed a proper hermeneutical discipline.

Anabaptists believe that the New Testament interprets the Old Testament. More specifically, they will read the Old Testament through the lens of Christ. Jesus fulfills the Law and the Prophets and, as such, presents the believer with the final standard of life and conduct for the Christian. When Anabaptists read the Old Testament and the New Testament, they interpret each in a way consistent with the revelation of God in Christ Jesus.[62] With Jesus as the lens through which believers examine the text, the natural gravitation will be to those texts that strongly portray his life and teachings. Other texts must be interpreted in light of these clearer texts.[63] Because the Anabaptist concern is for the ethical and ecclesiological issues of the church, their focus tends to be on the New Testament over the Old Testament.

Will the preference for the New Testament over the Old present a problem for the Anabaptist understanding of God's character? If the Anabaptists do not develop a hermeneutic for interpreting the Old Testament and the revelation of God therein, they may risk falling into the heresy of Marcionism. Their pacifist stance and their understanding of the God of grace conflicts with the God of the Old Testament, who commands his people to make war on the idolatrous nations. Yet in the same pages are revealed the God of grace who calls Israel back to himself, who presents himself as a loving husband willing to receive home his adulterous wife (Hosea). Preference for the New Testament impoverishes their understanding of the plan of salvation that streams through both Testaments.

Anabaptists further believe that the purpose of studying the Bible goes beyond knowledge, that it is a book for life. In other words, they study the Bible to become disciples. To that end, Anabaptists insist that the teachings of Scripture, specifically the Gospels, were meant to be followed. Even more specifically, Anabaptists take seriously the Sermon on the Mount as an ethic for this present age rather than the coming age as some evangelicals have thought. Avoiding the confusion of academic theology and sophisticated arguments regarding interpretation, they opt for a simple meaning of the text. They feel the Bible was not meant to be debated, but to be lived.[64]

Jesus' sermon in Matthew 5 to 7 must be obeyed as all Scripture must. But do the Anabaptists take the Sermon on the Mount too literally? Adhering to certain Scriptures over others may logically lead to legalism as those texts be-

---

62 Roth, 45.
63 Murray.
64 Roth, 46.

come the standard for Christianity. Mennonites have been inclined to legalistic interpretations of the Bible to the extent that they have isolated themselves as possessing the only truth and alienating other Christian perspectives. While there are clearly admirable elements to this Christocentrism, a focus on Christ as the pinnacle of God's revelation for one, their methodology and outworking of the principle may actually veer off of Christ and focus more on works.

Anabaptists and Biblical Inerrancy

An issue of contention between evangelicals and Anabaptists regarding the Bible exists concerning biblical inerrancy. In October 1978, more than two hundred evangelical leaders met at a conference in Chicago to formulate a statement on biblical inerrancy known as the Chicago Statement on Biblical Inerrancy (CSBI). The purpose of this statement was to assist evangelicals in defending the Bible against liberal trends that apparently eroded faith in the Bible as an infallible revelation of God's Word.

Of particular importance to this discussion was point number four under a summary called "A Short Statement." This declaration stated,

> Being wholly and verbally God-given, Scripture is without error or fault in all its teaching, no less in what it states about God's acts in creation, about the events of world history, and about its own literary origins under God, than in its witness to God's saving grace in individual lives.[65]

This is one of nineteen affirmations and denials that clarify what is meant by biblical inerrancy. Essentially, the writers of this document state that inspiration cannot accommodate error.

If there were errors in the written text of the Bible, according to CSBI, it would cease to be an inspired text. However, the conference went further by expanding the scope of biblical infallibility to include its truthfulness beyond that of spiritual and religious issues. As Article XII states,

> We deny that biblical infallibility and inerrancy are limited to spiritual, religious, or redemptive themes, exclusive of assertions in the fields of history and science. We further deny that scientific hypotheses about earth history may properly be used to overturn the teaching of Scripture on creation and the flood.

---

65 "The Chicago Statement on Biblical Inerrancy."

The thrust of this statement underscores the ideology that if a biblical author wrote that the world is flat, then it is flat. Taking Genesis 1-11 as an example, the CSBI commits evangelical hermeneutics to interpret this origin text as scientific, not just theological.

A careful study of the history of biblical inerrancy reveals a few holes in the theory. While inerrantists claim their view has been around since the early church, the word "inerrancy" itself is found nowhere in the Bible. The Bible uses terms such as "God-breathed" and refers to the Scriptures as "true and trustworthy," but the term "inerrant" is a theological interpretation applied to the text. Even the word "inerrant" has only been around since the nineteenth century, according to Wyatt Houtz.[66]

Anabaptists do not hold to the view of inerrancy. Biblical inerrancy implies that every single verse is inspired and should not be questioned. If one verse is questioned, then the integrity of the entire Bible would be called into question. The Bible is certainly a record of God's actions in history, and Mennonites believe this. They also believe in 2 Timothy 3:16, that Scripture is inspired, but this does not mean they apply the authority of Scripture to every issue, including science and astronomy. Does a historical, scientific, or geographical error in the text detract from the inspired nature of the Scriptures? If we accept that the biblical author of Genesis wrote from his own context and understanding with a limited scientific, or even primitive, understanding of astronomy, does the message of the text suffer? Anabaptists would say no.

Evangelicals who held to the CSBI were keen to keep the waters of liberalism from crashing through the walls of orthodoxy. They felt the only way to do this was to believe in the infallibility of the original autographs, the actual document that Matthew or John or Paul applied ink to, and that they were true in every fact and detail. The only problem with this view is that no original autographs exist and cannot verify such a claim; all we have is copies of copies of copies.

Anabaptists insist that the Bible need not be inerrant to be a fully trustworthy source for the Christian faith. They love the Scriptures and encourage the reading, memorizing, study, and contemplation of the many Bible passages. Again, the Bible is central to the Anabaptist faith, but they believe it makes no claim to inerrancy. The closest Mennonites comes to such a belief is found in various statements of faith which state, "We believe that the Bible is the Word of God. It is inspired by God and is without error in all it teaches. It is the final authority in matters of belief and conduct."[67] Note the subtle way

---

[66] Wyatt Houtz, "Biblical Inerrancy's Myth-Making Machine, Unveiled," http://postbarthian.com/2017/01/26/errors-inerrancy-7-biblical-inerrancy-myth-making-machine-unveiled/
[67] Evangelical Mennonite Conference statement of Faith Article 1.

the conference declares that the Bible is "without error in all that it teaches." It does not suggest or imply that the text is without error, but that the teaching of the Bible is without error. A fine line to be sure, but a notable foxtrot around a controversial issue with many Christians.

Biblical inerrancy is a much larger issue than can be addressed in this chapter on hermeneutics. If evangelicals and Anabaptists could agree that the Bible remains the authority for life and faith, that it provides guidance, comfort, and inspiration to followers of Christ in all situations, then they can proceed to cooperate in proclaiming the message of power and hope found in Christ.

Evangelicals and Anabaptists agree on the need for a biblical foundation to Christian faith and conduct. They agree that the Bible is inspired by God as he led the writers to convey a message that revealed God's will and character to a people who would be shaped by his decrees. There may be disagreements concerning biblical inerrancy, but these issues need not be divisive when both streams agree on the authority of what Scripture tells them. Anabaptists can learn from evangelicals about developing a biblical theology; evangelicals can learn from Anabaptists about making the Scriptures practical for life.

Chapter Four:
How We Understand the Atonement

The biblical message of atonement, God's provision of a way for humankind to return to God and have a harmonious relationship with him, is an important theological truth for all Christians. From Genesis through Revelation, God has revealed his desire to reconcile with humankind. The pinnacle of this effort to bring humankind back into relationship with himself is the sacrifice of Christ on the cross. No other act in history has achieved what the cross represents in reconciling us to God.[68] Atonement, the forgiveness of sins through the death of Jesus, is clearly the act of God throughout the Bible, something humankind was powerless to achieve.

Over the course of history, Christians have attempted to explain the death of Jesus as an atonement for sins and how it was efficacious for all with different metaphors. Gustaf Aulen's (1879-1978) *Christus Victor* was influential in understanding these various models. Scholars took these metaphors and grouped them as classical, objective, and subjective paradigms. Classical models included the Ransom Theory of atonement, which teaches that the death of Christ was a ransom sacrifice paid to Satan or death, and the Recapitulation Theory, which says that Christ accomplished what Adam could not. Aulen built on the Ransom Theory but argued that Christ's death was not a payment to the devil. Instead, Christ defeated the powers of evil on the cross, which had held humankind in bondage to sin. Aulen called this theory Christus Victor.

Objective models taught essentially three theories: The Satisfaction Theory, the Penal Substitution Theory, and the Moral Government Theory. The Satisfaction Theory taught that Jesus suffered crucifixion as a substitute for human sin, thereby satisfying God's righteous wrath against human sinfulness. Penal Substitution was a Reformation Era development from Anselm's Satisfaction Theory, as noted above, that saw Christ take the place of sinful humankind, bearing their place on the cross. Though the difference is slight between the two theories, it is noteworthy. The Satisfaction Theory focused on satisfying God's wrath for human sin, while Penal Substitution saw Christ taking the place of sinful persons on the cross. The Moral Government The-

---

[68] "Atonement – Baker's evangelical Dictionary of Biblical Theology Online." Bible Study Tools. Accessed March 27, 2019. http://www.Biblestudytools.com/dictionaries/bakers-evangelical-dictionary/atonement.html.

ory viewed God as the loving creator and governor of the universe and the atonement as appeasing God in his divine role as King of the Universe. This theory is typically taught in Arminian circles.

Subjective theories of the atonement include the Moral Influence Theory and the Moral Example Theory. The former theory was developed by Abelard (1079-1142), who proposed that Jesus died as a demonstration of God's love. That demonstration in itself was seen as effective in changing the hearts and minds of sinners, bringing them back to God. The latter theory follows closely to the former, emphasizing the example of Christ's self-sacrifice over the theory of vicarious satisfaction.

When we consider the various theories, can we apply one theory to evangelicalism and another to Anabaptism? Are the differences so stark that we can create a divide theologically between the two streams of thought?

Stereotyping a class of people or a movement such as the evangelicals or the Anabaptists only breeds misunderstanding and confusion. One can speak in generalities concerning what theory of atonement fits what camp, but there are always exceptions within the camps. Anabaptists, for instance, would have subscribed to the Classical theories at the time of the Reformation but have in the last decades been drawn to the Christus Victor theory of atonement. Being pacifists in practice, Christus Victor appeals to their nonviolent interpretation of Christ's life and death. Evangelicals, on the other hand, may fit more neatly into the Penal Substitution Theory given their fervor for evangelism and the appeal they make concerning the romantic imagery of a hero taking the place of the downtrodden. Again, that may be an oversimplification and an unfair classification.

What Anabaptists Believe About the Atonement

As noted above, placing Anabaptists into a particular box concerning the atonement and other theological issues has not been an easy task. Frances Hiebert identified several difficulties facing the development of Anabaptist theology beginning in the sixteenth century.[69]

First, Hiebert rehearsed the tribulation that Anabaptists experienced following the Peasants' War and the Muenster Tragedy. These episodes painted Anabaptists in a critically dark manner, making the name a byword for heresy in the Reformation era. Luther called his enemies "Anabaptists" even if they were not of that perspective. Consequently, writing theological treatises was

---

69 Frances F. Hiebert, *Direction: A Mennonite Brethren Forum.* Fall 2001 · Vol. 30 No. 2 · pp. 122–38.

not much of a priority, let alone developing doctrine, while being harried by magisterial authorities.

Then Hiebert addresses the umbrella term of Anabaptism, which masks a diversity among groups that bear that name. Given the geographical and social differences between the groups, there were bound to be varied approaches to this perspective. Some groups were in the Netherlands while others were in Austria, Hungary, Romania, and, of course, Switzerland. In addition, there were theological differences, however slight, between the groups, such as the orthodox Michael Sattler and the mystic-humanist Hans Denck.

Interpreting the Bible literally was a common hermeneutic of the Anabaptist perspective. But even here there were differences. Hutterites took the command to be separate from the world to the extreme by isolating themselves from society and forming communes or colonies to ensure that isolation. Mennonites were not as strict in retreating from the world in that manner but advocated for a disciplined community of faith. Life in a Mennonite community in the middle centuries could be quite rigid in adhering to the literal interpretation of Scripture, specifically the Sermon on the Mount.

Hiebert also noted the absence of unifying creeds among the Anabaptists. Though Sattler penned the Schleitheim Confession, giving some direction to the Swiss Anabaptists, it was by no means a creed or doctrinal statement. Their focus on Scripture as "all the creed we need" rejected other creeds as being of human invention. Menno Simons would not even heed the writings of the early church fathers unless what they wrote could be verified by Scripture.

So what position do Anabaptists take on the atonement? As with most theological themes, finding agreement among those who call themselves Anabaptists meets with inconclusive results. For the most part, Anabaptists agreed with the Reformers on matters of doctrine and made more practical interpretations where they differed. With respect to the atonement itself, Sattler believed the death of Christ was a propitiatory sacrifice offered to God to cover the sins of humanity.[70] It seems Anselm's Satisfaction Theory was acceptable to Anabaptists in the sixteenth century. At the same time, Anabaptists were comfortable using the language of three models of atonement: Classical, Satisfaction, and Christus Victor. They were naturally drawn to the Moral Example Theory since they believed strongly that Christ's example encouraged following him in obedience and suffering. And, as has been discussed earlier, geography played a part in the choice of model, as Dutch Anabaptists were

---

70 "Propitiation" refers to the need to appease God. Christ became our propitiation, the satisfaction that turned God's wrath away from sinful humankind.

particularly drawn to substitution language. In summary, Anabaptists were eclectic in their development of an atonement theory doctrine.

The Anabaptists differed with the Reformers concerning atonement in how it played out in the life of a believer. Anabaptists rejected salvation by works, or justification by law, as a means of salvation, but they did teach that once saved, the law was an important facet of living for Christ. This is not a reference to Old Testament law per se, but to what they called the Law of Christ written on their hearts. The works of faith were an important testimony to the fact of their salvation. Agreeing with the Satisfaction model, they also found it insufficient since it focused on Christ's death and reduced that death to a forensic doctrine, which only highlighted humanity's legal status before God. In other words, the Satisfaction model did not require any involvement from the human side of the equation.

Anabaptists felt that the atonement went beyond a new legal status before God. To them, it meant the oft-used and oversimplified "at-one-ment" with God in reference to the reconciling work of Christ on the cross.[71] Atonement meant more than status; it included not just the death of Christ but involved all aspects of Christ's work on behalf of humanity—his life, ministry, death, and resurrection. Thus, Anabaptists taught that unless a person responds appropriately to the work of Christ, the atonement is not efficacious. What Christ has done for humanity goes beyond saving them from sin; his work actualizes the power of the Holy Spirit so that those who begin to follow Christ in life are enabled to participate in his saving work. As a result, the gospel for Anabaptists was more than salvation, it was a series of directives for the Christian on how to live and follow the example of Christ. The Magisterial Reformers were quick to accuse them of emphasizing works over faith as a result.

The eclectic Anabaptist model of atonement insisted, however, that the atonement was the work of God through and through. God is the one who provides the means for salvation through the entire life of Jesus, the incarnation, the ministry, his death, and his resurrection. God calls the sinner to repent and accept the gospel. God restores the individual and empowers him or her to respond to the gospel of grace. Works-salvation was not on the table; works that expressed the response of the believing individual to God's work of grace was at stake.

---

71 "At-one-ment" is used to express how God and believing persons are now "at one" or reconciled.

Christus Victor

In these first decades of the twenty-first century, Anabaptists, in their writings and sermons, have moved significantly closer to the Christus Victor model of atonement. Their conflict with being "in the world, but not of it," the ongoing battle with the flesh and the devil, as well their consternation with religious and political structures, has given rise to the prominence of Christus Victor among Anabaptists. Since Christ came to destroy the work of the devil and the power of death and hell, Anabaptists see this model fitting these categories powerfully.

Christus Victor is Latin for "Christ the Victor." In the middle of the twentieth century, Gustaf Aulen, a theologian at the University of Lund in Sweden, wrote a book by the same title and brought the view back into Christian thinking. Christus Victor finds its roots in the early church's Ransom Theory, a popular understanding of Christ's death for the first thousand years of church history. According to Aulen, the classic Ransom Theory was not systematic theology so much as it was the passion story of God triumphing over evil powers and freeing humankind from the shackles of sin. Aulen wrote, "The work of Christ is first and foremost a victory over the powers that hold mankind in bondage: sin, death, and the devil."[72]

One issue with the Ransom Theory was the focus of the ransom. If Jesus died as a ransom for humanity held in bondage by sin, to whom was the ransom paid? A few presented the idea that Christ paid a direct ransom to Satan, though Satan was deceived as to the hidden clause in the transaction. Humankind was conquered by Satan through the sin of the fall and thus in bondage to Satan, the victor. When Satan accepted Christ as the ransom, he was unaware of the clause: Jesus could not be held because of his sinlessness. The imagery of Satan as a fish and Christ in human form as the bait on the invisible hook of Christ's divinity has been used to illustrate this transaction. Many object, even today, to the idea that Satan had the kind of bargaining power with God that he could demand a ransom. In response, a view developed that downplays the ransom being paid to Satan and simply states that Satan has power over humankind due to sin and that Christ conquered sin, breaking Satan's hold on humankind. The ransom is not paid to Satan, then, but simply breaks the power of sin, freeing humankind to follow Christ.

As an atonement theory, Christus Victor highlights some important scriptural truths that may be overlooked by other theories of atonement. In

---

72 Gustaf Aulen, *Christus Victor: An Historical Study of the Three Main Types of the Idea of Atonement*, trans. by A. G. Herber. Wipf & Stock, 2003. P. 20.

Christ's death and resurrection, Jesus did defeat and overthrow the dominion of Satan and achieve the release of humankind. The following texts support this aspect of the atonement:

> The reason the Son of God appeared was to destroy the works of the devil. (1 John 3:8).
>
> [God] having forgiven us all our trespasses, by canceling the record of debt that stood against us with its legal demands. This he set aside, nailing it to the cross. He disarmed the rulers and authorities and put them to open shame, by triumphing over them in him. (Colossians 2:13-15)
>
> Since therefore the children share in flesh and blood, he himself likewise partook of the same things, that through death he might destroy the one who has the power of death, that is, the devil, and deliver all those who through fear of death were subject to lifelong slavery. (Hebrews 2:14-15)

The Rise of the Satisfaction Theory of Atonement

When Anselm of Canterbury (1033-1109) published a book on his views of atonement focusing on the Satisfaction Theory, a major paradigm shift took place in the church. Anselm defined sin as humankind withholding from God the honor that belongs to God. Sin is therefore a debt, a failure to give God the obedience owed to him. That debt places an obligation on humankind to give to God full obedience in everything; to pay back the honor due to God that our sin robbed him of; and to pay back more than what was taken away because of the insult that dishonor inflicted on God. Humankind cannot pay back this obedience and honor because what God requires of humankind is already rightfully his, so they have nothing to offer. Sin itself presents a gross offense to God, who is infinitely holy and eternal; therefore, the satisfaction would also need to be eternal to satisfy an eternally righteous God.

Anselm theorized that God, who is full of love and mercy, could not simply dismiss the offense and forgive the sin. For if sin remains unpunished, the law would be rendered weak and ineffective, and those who adhered to the law would be no better off than the unrepentant sinner. Furthermore, to leave sin unpunished would make a mockery of God's justice, with humankind defrauding the Creator of what he was owed.

Humankind cannot make satisfaction on its own; God can pay the debt, but he does not owe the debt. How can satisfaction be made? Anselm proposed this answer:

> Satisfaction cannot be made unless there be some One able to pay God for man's sin something greater than all that is beside God... Now nothing is greater than all that is beside God except God himself. None therefore can make this satisfaction except God. And none ought to make it except man... If, then, it be necessary that the kingdom of heaven be completed by man's admission, and if man cannot be admitted unless the aforesaid satisfaction for sin be first made, and if God only can, and man only ought to make this satisfaction, then necessarily One must make it who is both God and man. (Book II, ch. 6)[73]

Only one who could represent humankind and at the same time represent God could bear the guilt and satisfy the debt of sin. The death of Christ on the cross thus honors God and covers the sins of women and men because Christ offered a gift to God that he did not owe but which was more than sufficient to pay for our sins. Jesus did not deserve to die but gave himself willingly to death, and this, Anselm stated, was beautiful in God's sight. Finally, Christ's death was unjust, but since Jesus endured this injustice willingly, the merit of his death was powerful and more than needed to pay for the sins of humankind.

The aforementioned paradigm shift in the church was the movement from the Ransom Theory toward the Satisfaction Theory put forth by Anselm. With the Reformation, Protestant theologians focused on Penal Substitutionary Atonement where satisfaction was achieved through vicarious suffering. Penal Substitution as a theory found its origins in the early church just as the Ransom Theory had, but the Reformers emphasized the satisfaction theory more fully through Penal Substitution. Modern evangelicals have subscribed to this theory more than other theories of the atonement.

If one takes the Penal Substitution theory by itself, some disturbing images arise, out of which comes a flood of questions. An image of a wrathful God who will not be satisfied until blood is spilled centers on violence as the answer to humankind's predicament with sin. Out of this picture emerges God as Father taking vengeance on his own Son instead of on those sinful humans, a kind of divine child abuse. We see the Father full of rage against sinners and Jesus standing in the place of sinners pleading with the Father to

---

[73] Sam Storms, "10 Things You Should Know about the Satisfaction Theory of the Atonement." https://www.samstorms.com/enjoying-god-blog/post/10-things-you-should-know-about-the-satisfaction-theory-of-the-atonement

take out his wrath on him. This image is not consistent with the Father and the Son of the Gospels, where Father and Son are in agreement about how to atone for sinners. Penal Substitution does not portray God as loving and compassionate but as a mean ogre, unapproachable and terribly angry that his honor has been maligned. Some have even suggested that violence is justified as a remedy to other problems in our world since God used violence on the cross to destroy sin and death.

Does God's Anger Need to Be Satisfied?

The evangelical evangelist has continuously motivated sinners to repent based on the fearful anger of God. Jonathan Edwards preached his "Sinners in the hands of an angry God" to a terrified crowd that could not wait to repent due to the fear that gripped their hearts. Some said it felt as though the fires of hell were licking at their feet beneath the very floor of the church. On into the twentieth century, the dynamic evangelists continued this theme, inviting sinners to escape the wrath of God. It is a prevalent theme, but is this God's character?

Popular impressions of the Old Testament are that these Scriptures depict a wrathful God while the New Testament gives us the gracious and merciful God. Yet when we read carefully the Old Testament accounts of God's anger, we see that it does not need to be removed as much as it is turned away, and this through repentance. For example, when David committed adultery with Bathsheba and murdered her husband, God was angry with David and confronted him through Nathan the prophet. Did God demand David's death as a result of his sin? No, but David repented before God and wrote the emotionally penitent Psalm 51 describing his confession to God. Despite this grievous sin, David continued to act as the template for the coming Messiah who would be known as "the Son of David."

God's wrath and judgment are not based on human configurations, whereby wrath must expend itself or God will explode. Penal Substitutionary Atonement promotes that idea in that God's wrath must be poured out on a target to satisfy his justice. Christ acts in our place to receive that wrath, according to PSA, because it must be spent on something or someone.

What removes, or better yet—overcomes, God's wrath? That would be mercy. James writes, "For judgment is without mercy to one who has shown no mercy. Mercy triumphs over judgment" (James 2:13). God is merciful and stands not with arms crossed but with arms open to receive the sinner. Martin Luther himself feared the angry God persona until he discovered the grace of God in the book of Romans.

The New Testament uses the language of sacrifice to describe the actions of God in relation to humankind. Passover imagery was covenant imagery, God delivering his people through the blood of the lamb. It was God's action. Day of Atonement imagery does move toward setting the house in order through the shedding of blood as an offering on behalf of God's people to God. Through Jesus' incarnation, God comes to and meets humankind at the mercy seat of God where the blood is shed for sins. God in Christ enters into humanity's mortality and death in order to destroy death. So rather than God seeking a target to pour his wrath upon, God sacrifices enormously to deliver humanity from the wrath of judgment.

Any other understanding of the atonement leads to imagery akin to a pagan ritual of sacrificing to the gods to placate their anger. With the New Testament understanding of atonement, God removes the wrath. Otherwise, God would be seen as killing Jesus to assuage his own anger at humanity.

The apostle Paul, reflecting on the work of Christ on the cross, did speak of substitution, but also of Christ's victory. To the Colossians, Paul wrote, "He disarmed the rulers and authorities and put them to open shame, by triumphing over them in him" (Colossians 2:15). Sin, death, and violence exhausted themselves completely on Jesus Christ when he hung upon the cross. That is what Paul meant by Christ disarming the rulers and the authorities; their violent methodology was broken and disgraced on the cross so that the world would see their emptiness. Sin, death, and violence did their worst to Jesus, and Jesus overcame them by his death and resurrection.

Christus Victor may appeal to Anabaptists because of its nonviolent emphasis, but the cross was an unavoidable act of violence. So what part do each of the participants play in this drama? Does God demand sacrifice? Was Jesus a willing victim? Do Jews and Gentiles bear an equal share in the death of Christ? One theory of atonement does not sufficiently reveal the entirety of the passion of Christ, but each one gives the church a perspective to meditate upon and proclaim. The church may need to move beyond these theories and develop a biblical and holistic theory of atonement. And as some readily confess, we are not saved by theories, but by the person of Jesus Christ. We will continue to wrestle with how that takes place until Christ comes.

Chapter Five:
Why Popular Eschatology Needs to Be "Left Behind"

North Americans love to read and watch movies about dystopian futures with zombies, alien invasions, or the collapse of society and the rise of "survivors." It would make for an intriguing study to plumb the depths of this American fascination with disaster scenarios where individuals and groups have to fight for their lives. Where did it begin? Why do certain types of people enjoy being afraid of the future? Unfortunately, we will not address the answers to these questions in this chapter. Our discussion of evangelicalism relates to the subject of dystopian literature and thought: rapture theology.

> The popularity of books like *The Late Great Planet Earth*, by Hal Lindsey, and the *Left Behind* series, by Tim LaHaye and Jerry B. Jenkins, serve to illustrate the American desire for futuristic literature. Novels by the latter authors are even read by those who do not count themselves as Christian but enjoy the drama and suspense of the series. Many will admit that the books are not well-written and will consequently add that perfect prose is not the point. For many readers, these novels are not just entertainment, but they are commentaries on the coming rapture and the new world that follows the great tribulation. For those who struggle to read their Bibles and interpret the texts, the Left Behind books provide a readable window into the enigmatic apocalyptic literature of the Bible. Through popular literature, evangelical Christians have been indoctrinated to believe it is the only doctrine that answers the question: What happens next?

There are various names for this doctrine: rapture theology, dispensationalism, or Premillennialism, among others. For the past two centuries, North American evangelicalism has been enraptured by this interpretation of end-times theology. The majority of institutes of higher biblical education have taught this eschatological perspective in their curriculums for the past century, and only recently have Bible scholars of a different bent begun to present alternative viewpoints of the End.[74] However, rapture theology has been so entrenched in the minds of the Revival Generation that to preach another doctrine on Daniel, Revelation, or eschatology is to meet with the wrath of disturbed congregants who want or need a rapture before the great tribulation.

Rapture theology or dispensationalism did not enter mainstream Christianity until the middle of the nineteenth century. The word "rapture" is itself an invention of John Nelson Darby and does not have roots in the Bible. Odd, then, that evangelicals who are sticklers for being biblically informed would grasp on to an unbiblical doctrine.

How did rapture theology enter evangelical thinking?

Timeline of "Rapture" Theology

The modern evangelical movement finds its roots in the early colonial America era of the seventeenth century, with its emphasis on experiential conversion and faith. This period was characterized by an intense time of preaching about the need for a saving Christ and a rejection of merely formal religion that characterized the church of England in the minds of the Puritans. The Puritan movement imagined itself as finishing the work of the English Reformation and purifying the church.[75]

> *Increase Mather*: Increase Mather (1639-1723), pastor of a church in Boston, Massachusetts, was a proponent of the principles of conversion as a work of the Holy Spirit, the life of holiness as the expectation of every Christian, evangelization of every class, and agencies promoting the work of God in the world. These specific principles would later inspire and form the foundations for evangelicals in their doctrinal foundations. Wilbur Smith noted that the Puritans had a powerful influence over the religious underpinnings of early America: "The Puritans were the greatest theologians, all in all, that our country has ever seen. It probably is no exaggeration to say that they have exerted more influence over the religious and theological thinking of the Republic of the United States than any other single body of men."[76] Indeed, during the long tenure of the Mathers, there

---

74 Sam Storms presents amillennial alternatives to the predominant premillennial perspective.
75 Noll, *The Rise of Evangelicalism*, 53.
76 Wilbur M. Smith, "The Prophetic Literature of Colonial America," *Bibliotheca Sacra* 100, no. 397 [January-March, 1943]: 67.

endured a strong piety among the Puritans until prosperity began to erode the commitment of many Puritans to holy living.77

Nevertheless, Increase Mather had a profound effect on the Puritan understanding of biblical prophecy. Smith wrote that the first prophetic literature of importance in America was written by Mather.78 His first book, written in 1669, *The Mystery of Israel's Salvation Explained and Applied, or a discourse concerning the general conversion of the Israelitish Nation*, was a treatise on Chiliastical teachings.79 He writes concerning his convictions on four principles: that the thousand-year reign is not past, but future; that the coming of Christ to raise the dead and judge the earth precedes the millennium; that the conversion of the Jews will take place just before the end of the world; and that the Jewish conversion will be a glorious day for the believers at the end of time.80 A great emphasis is placed upon the Jews converting to Christianity, though Mather believed that the time of this conversion was imminent. Rapture theology continues to put great stock in the belief that God's chosen people, the Jews, will be saved and become great evangelists in the latter days. The origin of this belief can be seen in Mather's four principles.

A brief snapshot of Mather's reasoning and hermeneutics are evident in the following words:

As when Israel was redeemed out of Egypt, they were in a most forlorn, and seemingly forever undone estate according to that Scripture (Ezek. 16:5), so must it be with them again before this their great deliverance (Jer. 30:7). Yet I am persuaded that after the Israelites shall be in their own Land again, they shall be brought into the greatest distress that ever any people were in this world (Daniel 12:1; Joel 3:1, 2; Zech. 12:2, 3, 14:1-12; Rev. 16:14, 15; Mai. 4:1-3)... Before this salvation is over the great battle of Armageddon must be fought which will be the most terrible day of battle that ever was... There is reason to hope that the salvation of the Tribes of Israel is near to be revealed... that the latter part of these days are accomplished in

---

77 Noll, *The Rise of Evangelicalism*, 71.
78 Smith, "The Prophetic Literature of Colonial America," 74.
79 "Chiliasm" is another term for the doctrine of the thousand-year period of peace and prosperity.
80 Smith, "The Prophetic Literature of Colonial America," 76.

> some measure is evident if we consider the character of the last times laid down by the Apostle Paul (2 Tim. 3).[81]

One redeeming aspect of Mather's understanding of apocalyptic literature is that he refused to set dates for any of these fulfilments of biblical prophecy. He wrote,

> An infallible demonstration of the exact time when Israel shall be saved cannot be given. After men have said all that they can say about this matter, all is but a human conjecture, and not an infallible definite conclusion, as to the day, month or year when this salvation shall have its effect. I cannot, for my own part by searching, find out that the particular year when the Jews shall be converted is anywhere in all the Scripture once mentioned… No one can tell justly when the day of judgment shall begin, for none can tell justly how old the world is.[82]

Later preachers building on Mather's teaching would not be so wise, as certain evangelicals delighted in setting dates or attempting to interpret the times by natural and political catastrophes. Evangelicals enamored with eschatological yearnings tied these catastrophes or world events to Scriptures that, in their opinion, pointed to signs of Christ's second coming, the tribulation, or any number of related themes and predictions. These predictions offered little in terms of credibility for the cause of Christ since date-setting and interpretations of historical events fell flat, leaving the interpreter of the signs without his proof.

Mather believed Chiliasm was the deep conviction of the church from the beginning and that it was dropped during Constantine, though he gives little explanation for the reason it was dropped.[83] As with many such doctrines, proponents of these themes delight in proclaiming that the theology in question is ancient. This may be a matter of interpretation and wishful thinking. During the first three centuries, the church was under intense persecution and, consequently, employed an attitude of imminence concerning the return of Christ. They found their hope in suffering through the promise of Christ's return and will have interpreted their context in apocalyptic terms, seeing Rome as Revelation's Babylon and Caesar as the antichrist. Revelation continues to be the favorite book of those believers suffering persecution today given its hope in the midst of suffering and loss. When Christianity was

---

81   Ibid, 77.
82   Ibid, 80.
83   Ibid, 78.

legalized as a religion under Constantine, the persecution ceased and Christians may not have looked as longingly for Christ's return. The question we cannot answer is whether the early Christians were Chiliasts.

In keeping with his understanding of the role of Israel in the end times, Mather believed that a great revival at the end of the age would fall upon all mankind; all Israel shall be saved, unconverted Gentiles… "even amongst Indians, Infidels and such as never heard the name of Jesus."[84] The twenty-first-century lens with which we view history these days will quickly pick up the racist tones of Mather's comments. "Even amongst Indians" suggests they are the least likely to be saved by the gospel. But it is possible under God's gracious hand, Mather would reply. In his context, Mather may not be faulted for thinking this way, though we find such comments repugnant. His ethics come under further scrutiny when we study his involvement in the Salem Witch Trials. At first, it seemed Mather found the trials unjust, but then we read how he found the trial of one fellow acceptable and his execution justifiable. His hope of a future revival, then, asks what regeneration would look like in the new believer and how he saw the new ethic in himself.

A further critique of Mather and his understanding of the Christian life is warranted. However, our concern is that his writings provided a base for future evangelicals to form an eschatology. For that theme, we turn to John Nelson Darby.

> *John Nelson Darby* (1800-1882): Darby, born in London to a prominent family, first became a lawyer and then a priest in the church of Ireland. Only two years into his tenure as a minister, he became concerned with the poor condition of the church and its lifeless formality. He left that church and helped found a non-denominational group called the Brethren, later known as the Plymouth Brethren. He desired a simpler church and a "priesthood of believers" where each member served as a minister.

In laying out the beliefs of the Brethren Church, Darby produced a pamphlet explaining those beliefs, including the teaching of premillennialism and dispensationalism. Darby, with dispensationalism, attempted to explain why God's work in the different parts of the Bible and in history seemed to differ. He also taught that the church was not the New Israel, but that they were distinct, with Israel continuing to play a significant role in the future. The seven dispensations he devised broke history into divisions: Paradise, Noah,

---

84 Ibid, 81.

Abraham, Israel, Gentiles, the Spirit, and the Millennium. Darby's interpretation of Scripture was quite literal, a departure from the predominant interpretations of the era. He thus saw Israel and the church as separate, and the rapture and the second coming as two different events.

Darby may be most noted for his theory of the "secret rapture," which posits the belief that Christ will come to take believers out of the world before returning with them at the second coming. No one will see Jesus coming to receive these believers except the believers, which is why it is called "secret." Then Jesus will come again and the whole world will see him, according to this doctrine (Revelation 1:7). Many found the theory controversial in the mid-nineteenth century, even among premillennialists. As the theory developed into the pretribulation rapture theory, it became more popular, though it still caused ripples in the faith community.[85] Even so, the secret rapture remains popular today, as writers like Hal Lindsey, Tim LaHaye, and Jerry Jenkins have brought the doctrine into the mainstream of popular culture with their books and novels.

Anyone reading the Scriptures for themselves may find it difficult to identify the "secret" rapture. As one early writer said,

> There is not a Bible teacher or anyone else living in the world today who has found a secret rapture in the Bible by his own independent study of the Bible itself. These teachers come to the Bible with cut and dried theories which they have learned elsewhere, and twist and torture texts to fit the theory.

Evangelicals have become more knowledgeable concerning theology and Bible study in the past couple of decades and have begun to question the position. Even evangelical scholars are not as enthusiastic as they once were. Michael Svigel confesses, "The perception among interested exegetes and theologians appears to be that rapture theology rests not on verifiable exegesis but on inferences drawn from ambiguous biblical passages and on peculiar dispensational presuppositions. In short, many today believe that the doctrine of the church's rapture from the earth prior to the seven-year tribulation period simply has no clear exegetical basis."[86] Though Svigel supports rapture theology, his comments regarding evangelical scholars are worth noting.

---

85 Michael J. Svigel, "'What Child Is This?': Darby's Early Exegetical Argument for the Pretribulation Rapture of the Church," *Trinity Journal*, vol. 35, issue 2 [January 1, 2014]: 225.
86 Ibid, 226.

Darby appealed to an exegetical argument from Revelation 12:5 as the basis for his teaching on the pretribulation rapture, where the entire church will be caught up prior to the so-called seven-year tribulation. He attached a corporate identification to the male child of that passage, proposing that the child is Christ mystically united with the church. Darby based this interpretation on a fourfold presupposition: a futurist interpretation of Apocalyptic literature and of the seventieth week of Daniel 9:27; the aforementioned mystical union of Christ and the church; distinguishing Israel from the church; and a literal understanding of the timestamps of Revelation 11-13. These indicators convinced Darby that the rapture of the church in 1 Thessalonians 4:17 would occur before the great tribulation, a seven-year time of difficulty for the world.[87]

For Darby, Revelation 12:5 referred not to historical or prophetic events but to the general relationship of the church in God's plan. The woman in the vision represented the spiritual position of the church in Christ in that general sense. "Having been born from the woman (Israel), the male child (the church) is described in terms of the King Messiah in whose image this corporate body is to be conformed."[88] As the text continues, the woman is threatened and pursued into the wilderness; this is the actual historical experience of the people of God, as Darby saw it. Before the woman is swallowed by the dragon, the woman (the church) is caught up to God, where she will be safe for the remainder of the tribulation. In respect to the timing of this event, Darby believed the church period rested between the sixty-ninth and seventieth weeks mentioned by Daniel (Daniel 9:24-27). During the sixty-ninth week, Christ comes to earth as a man and is killed, Darby states, and receives nothing. That is, he does not receive the church to himself but works to gather to himself those who would believe in his name. These faithful ones will be "caught up" at the beginning or before the seventieth week.[89] The seventieth week translates, according to premillennial eschatology, as the seven-years tribulation. Darby pins this event in history by saying,

> I have read this chapter of the Revelation, in order to show that while one class of persons—those associated with Christ—are caught up to God and there is triumph and rejoicing and gladness amongst them when Satan is cast down, that is the very time when tribulation begins on the earth.[90]

---

87   Svigel, 228.
88   Ibid, 232.
89   John Nelson Darby, *Lectures on the second coming* (London: G. Morrish, 1909), 54-61.
90   Darby, 68.

In his interpretation, the church does not figure strongly in the book of Revelation and the terrible scenes of wrath, except for this rapture, which are all in the future. His exegesis does not allow for the original readers of Revelation to see themselves as the subject of these visions and events. More will be said about this faulty hermeneutic later, but it bears highlighting at this point that a solely futuristic reading of Revelation tends to minimize its relevance for the present sufferer.

Darby may rightly be credited with inventing the rapture theology. His work on describing the rapture has been attached popularly with dispensational or premillennial theology from the mid-nineteenth century on to the present. Various scholars of the dispensational inclination have built on Darby's foundation and carried it on, refining it and promoting it until it became the de facto position of most evangelicals. Rapture theology continues to inform evangelical evangelism and its global worldview. Through the fundamentalist movement, and later the evangelical movement, Anabaptists forsook their original position for this popular theology so that it began to inform how Anabaptists saw the world in the twentieth century.

Rapture theology enjoys this popularity even though it finds no solid foundation in post-apostolic writings. Investigating writers like Papias (70-163 AD), who gathered the sayings of Jesus into a chronicle, books such as 1 and 2 Clement, the Epistle of Barnabas, the Didache, Ignatius, and so on reveal that pretribulational, dispensational premillennialism did not exist in the post-apostolic era. When you attempt to find rapture theology in the same writings, you will find no concept of rapture in them or in *The Shepherd of Hermas* or Polycarp. They do not even give a hint of the church passing through the tribulation as a separate event.[91]

Rapture theology is peculiar because of its inconsistent hermeneutical style, interpreting some biblical texts literally and others figuratively with no apology given except that it fits their interpretation. For a Bible-loving movement, one would expect the evangelical hermeneutic to examine this theology more carefully. Instead, it seems that rapture theology begins with a position and applies it to the text.

> *Hal Lindsey* (1929 -): Lindsey is an American evangelist and author of several books, including *The Late Great Planet Earth* (1970), which has sold over 35 million copies worldwide. Many of Lindsey's books written after *Late Great Planet Earth* (LGPE) are sequels, variations, or revisions of this seminal book. Lindsey continues to promote his

---

91 Sam Storms, *Kingdom Come* (Ross-Shire, Scotland: Mentor, 2013), 173.

brand of dispensationalism through his website and produces various conspiracy theories involving Russia, the European Union, or the political maneuverings of liberal politicians in the US. He is constantly searching for clues as to the identity of the antichrist.

Lindsey's teaching falls under the umbrella of Darby, C. I. Scofield, Lewis Sperry Chafer, and others who have taught rapture theology. Often called "popular eschatology," Lindsey's LGPE has largely influenced fundamentalist-evangelical theology at the lay level and even seeped into Anabaptist circles along with fundamentalist tendencies. Since fundamentalism was a reaction to Modernism, eschatology was one of the walls of the fortress set up to keep Modernism at bay. Any Christian doctrine that opposes the dispensational position of the Bible has, as a result, often been labeled "liberal." A conservative Christian will naturally cling to rapture theology in the face of those forces that seek to erode the authority of the Scriptures, they say.

The rise of LGPE in popularity among evangelicals and Anabaptists had a lot to do with the wars Israel fought in the 1960s and the Six-Day War in particular. All eyes turned to the Middle East to see if the newly created state of Israel with its persistent conflicts with Muslim neighbors would usher in the end times. Lindsey offered predictions, or prophecies, using biblical texts to shed light on current events as he interpreted them. At a time when the world worried about global conflict, Lindsey gave his readers hope concerning the future from an evangelical biblical perspective. He did this through outlining the Old Testament (OT) track record on fulfilled prophecy and offering them as proof of the reliability of biblical prophecy.

Lindsey found evidence for prophetic fulfillment in the writings of Micah and the remarkably precise Psalm 22 and Isaiah 53 in relation to Christ. Since these prophecies concerning Christ were so clearly fulfilled, other OT prophecies such as the return to Israel of God's people in the latter days must be verifiable as well. And what clearer evidence than the Zionist movement and the creation of the state of Israel in 1948, says Lindsey.[92] This provides the basis for other revelations concerning the future, including Gog and Magog in Ezekiel's prophecy and their connection to Russian and Moscow.[93] Lindsey's literal hermeneutic goes on from there to make outrageous and unsubstantiated connections from OT prophecies to current events, thus creating a grim portrait of what is yet to be.

Interpreting the course of history, Lindsey's summary of events followed

---

92   Marlin Jeschke "Pop Eschatology: Hal Lindsey and Evangelical Theology," *Evangelicalism and Anabaptism*, 126.
93   Hal Lindsey, *The Late Great Planet Earth* (New York: Bantam, 1974), 146.

this path:

- Believers in all ages have awaited the second coming of Christ. The early church fathers expected a millennial reign on the earth, which would be a return to paradise.
- When Augustine wrote the *City of God* in the fifth century, the expectation of the millennial reign as a literal experience on the earth morphed into the reign of Christ as represented in the hearts of believers as opposed to a future kingdom. The Roman Catholic Church specifically envisioned the rule of Christ taking place through the church, especially following the fall of the Roman Empire. The pope represented the reign of Christ through his office.
- When the Reformers began to separate from the Roman Catholic Church, they also modified the eschatological scheme. They concurred that the first thousand years of church history did represent the reign of Christ, but that the second millennium of church history saw the apostatizing of the church under the papacy, who they believed was the antichrist.
- Following the Reformation and the success of the Reformers in renewing the church and its theology, a new interpretation emerged of eschatology in which Armageddon, the final battle marking the end of the world, would occur in 1666.
- With the advent of science in the next centuries, the envisioned hope of the millennial reign of Christ shifted again. Many began to believe that the millennium of Christ would be ushered in by science and reason rather than through severe legislation.
- The French Revolution shattered everyone's menagerie of idealism and again shifted the paradigm of eschatology. When the horror of the French king being guillotined made news in England, theological students believed they were observing the first of the ten kings of Revelation being dethroned. And with the rise of Napoleon, they thought they were witnessing the rise of the antichrist.
- Then the dawning of the nineteenth century saw the emergence of dispensationalism in England. The popularity of this school of thought became the basis upon which Hal Lindsey formulated the popular eschatology of the twentieth century.

Lindsey's eschatology builds upon Darby's secret rapture theory and Israel's place in world history. It involves a literal seven-year tribulation and a literal thousand-year reign of Christ following the tribulation. Lindsey asks his readers where they want to be when the suffering and bloodshed of the tribulation occurs and tells them it is up to them to believe or not. The rapture is the escape hatch from a world doomed to destruction; a lifeboat for those on the sinking S.S. World. Lindsey admits the reader will not find "rapture" in the Bible, but it is clearly depicted and explained in Scripture. Rapture figures prominently as the only escape from tribulation in this scheme.

> The word "rapture" means to snatch away or take out...Someday, a day that only God knows, Jesus Christ is coming to take away all those who believe in him. He is coming to meet all true believers in the air. Without the benefit of science, space suits, or interplanetary rockets, there will be those who will be transported into a glorious place more beautiful, more awesome, than we can possibly comprehend. Earth and all its thrills, excitement, and pleasures will be nothing in contrast to this great event.[94]

Darby's secret rapture theory had been set aside by many premillennialists in the nineteenth century, but Lindsey made it popular again. That secrecy is underlined in his words, "The world will not know what has happened, because it occurs in an atom of time."[95] Lindsey bases the rapture on the premillennial interpretation of 1 Corinthians 15:51, 2 Corinthians 5:1-10, and 1 Thessalonians 4:13-18. The Thessalonians text is one of the most direct when speaking of "meeting the Lord in the air," which Lindsey connects to rapture.

Whereas Darby did not attempt to predict when the rapture and other events of the Apocalypse would occur. Lindsey "connected the dots" of the prophetic timeline and came up with a prediction. Many who read Lindsey's LGPE expected Jesus to return in the 1980s, some even suggesting May 14, 1988. This dating was reasoned from Matthew 24:32-34, where Jesus said his disciples were to learn from the fig tree and interpret the times. Jesus then said, "This generation will certainly not pass away until all these things have happened." If the fig tree represents Israel, its budding referred to the state of Israel being created on May 14, 1948. Since a generation is supposedly forty years, that puts the date at 1988. The rapture would take place seven years prior, Christians would escape the seven-years tribulation, and May 14, 1981 would be the beginning of the end. Of course, none of that happened.

Tim LaHaye and Jerry B. Jenkins: Hal Lindsey may not be the household name among millennial evangelicals that he was among Boomers of the 70s,

---

94 Lindsey, *Late Great Planet Earth*, 126.
95 Ibid, 131.

but his brand of eschatology found resurgence through the popular *Left Behind* books of Tim LaHaye and Jerry B. Jenkins. Between 1995 and 2007, this writing team wrote sixteen fictional novels based on rapture theology and other premillennial themes. Most critics agree that the writing and the plot are a poor example of literature. Even as they are recognized as fiction, not theology, many who prefer to receive their "knowledge" from Christian fiction than from the Bible received these novels as gospel.

The books follow the premillennial understanding of the end times, including the rise of the antichrist, the plagues of Revelation, the seven years tribulation, and, of course, the rapture. These are portrayed through the eyes of the main protagonists, Rayford Steele and Buck Williams. Steele and Williams are "left behind" and are forced to deal with the ongoing events of the tribulation. The two men become part of a "Tribulation Force" and begin to resist the mark of the beast while waiting for Jesus to come back.

What is the appeal of a series of novels that are actually more popular than the Harry Potter series? In short, escapism. When current events, such as the Middle East crisis of the 1990s, the terrorist attack on the World Trade Center in 2001, or the increasing unrest in the political and financial realms of the world become overwhelming, people search for a way out. Some imagine aliens coming to earth to reveal new technologies or answers to human dilemmas; others, like evangelical Christians, turn to rapture theology. As Charles Anderson opined,

> The Left Behind Series suggests that you too can be the winner of the great Prize in the Sky. Escape from this world of woe to be with those you love in heaven! The worse one can make the woe of the world appear, the greater the longing for escape.[96]

He goes on to say that the real strength of Christianity lies not in the offer of a miraculous escape from the troubles of this world but in the inspiration to resist them.

Rapture theology may be a recent invention of John Nelson Darby and his impoverished hermeneutic, but the evangelical world largely believes it because of writers like LaHaye and Jenkins. They appealed to the fears of Christians who abhor the idea of suffering and desperately hope that by believing in Jesus, they might escape something worse. Whenever a world event of cataclysmic potential threatens peace and security, rapture theology gains renewed attention.

---

96 Charles Anderson, "The Left Behind Series: Bad Fiction, Bad Faith." http://www.godweb.org/leftbehind.htm.

Anabaptist Resistance to Dispensational Theology

Where evangelicals have primarily proclaimed dispensationalism, or rapture theology, Anabaptists have resisted this interpretation of Scripture. Dispensational theology emphasizes the kingdom, but it portrays the kingdom of God as almost completely future.[97] By way of contrast, Anabaptists believe that the kingdom of God is actually found in the "now" while confessing that it is also "not yet." In other words, Anabaptists are not waiting for a millennium when the kingdom will come; they believe they are living under the reign of Christ now. Anabaptists are not anticipating the seven-year tribulation of the church in which believers will be persecuted for their allegiance to Christ; they believe that the tribulation began when Christ was resurrected and the church was born. The kingdom is now.

Though dispensational or rapture theology has become widespread, even among Anabaptists, there are critical concerns with the theory from an Anabaptist perspective. We will examine the predominate conflicts with Anabaptist thinking.

The Kingdom in Anabaptist Understanding: First, Anabaptists view the kingdom of God as a present reality with a future fulfillment. When reading the gospel according to Matthew, Christians are introduced to a strong sense of kingdom theology. Jesus preached from the mount, "Seek first the kingdom of God" (Matthew 6:33), thereby emphasizing the primacy of the kingdom of God. Christians are to seek this kingdom in the present age.

One enters the kingdom of God through repentance. When Jesus began his ministry, he declared, "The time is fulfilled and the kingdom of God is at hand; repent and believe the gospel" (Mark 1:15). Through repentance of sin and belief in Christ as the One who takes away the sins of the world, we enter the reality of the kingdom of God. Jesus is the King of this kingdom, which is why the Apostles called him Lord.[98] Putting one's faith in Jesus like this changes one's allegiance, outlook, values, and ethics from the kingdom of darkness to the kingdom of God.

---

[97] Paul M. Lederach, *A Third Way* (Scottdale, PA: Herald Press, 1980), 32.
[98] Behind the idea of "kingdom" is that Jesus is King. When we say, "Jesus is Lord," we are declaring that Jesus is King. Other titles are more or less direct but convey the same idea: "King of Israel" (John 1:49), "Son of David" (Matthew 1:1), "Son of God" (John 1:49), "Son of Man" (Christ's favorite self-designation based on Daniel 7:14 and found in the Gospels, especially Mark).

The transformation due to this new allegiance to Christ takes effect on how we live in the present age. We find the kingdoms in conflict, darkness, and light so that the world grows intolerant of Christian values. Believers will be persecuted, but their response is to be like Christ. "Those in the kingdom do not look forward to a time when swords will be beaten into plowshares, they already demonstrate that reality."[99] To be blunt, it means Christians do not retaliate to the violence of the world with violence but with peaceful responses in the same way Christ responded to his antagonists.

God works through the church to build his kingdom in the midst of a violent, godless world. The folksy stylings of the band *Rend Collective* preach a similar message when they sing, "Build your kingdom here; change the atmosphere," suggesting that the church builds the kingdom in the present. The kingdom exists in conflicted situations when the people who are called by God's name give love in the face of hatred, forgiveness and mercy in the face of hostility, and compassion in the face of greed. Even so, the conflict between the two kingdoms is a reality, and the challenge for Christ-followers is to remember we are citizens of heaven and do not give allegiance to world powers (Philippians 3:20).

Where is the kingdom? The Pharisees once asked Jesus this question. Jesus answered, "The kingdom of God is not coming in ways that can be observed, nor will they say, 'Look, here it is!' or 'There!' for behold, the kingdom of God is in the midst of you" (Luke 17:20-21). Some translations even say that the kingdom of God is "within you." From that perspective, we can say that the kingdom is not merely in the future, but it is a present reality. Jesus also said the casting out of demons was a sure sign that the kingdom of God had come: "But if it is by the Spirit of God that I cast out demons, then the kingdom of God has come upon you" (Matthew 12:28).

The Anabaptist concept of "kingdom" stands in opposition to the futuristic lens of rapture theology. This perspective makes imperative the call to be obedient to the Sermon on the Mount as the new ethic of the kingdom, which rapture theology places in the millennium to come. As a result, there is no expectation to "love your enemy" even at the cost of your life in dispensational theology.

Anabaptist Objections to rapture theology: As a theology, dispensationalism begins with the Old Testament and theorizes that the prophecies of the Old Testament about the kingdom have not been literally fulfilled. Fulfillment of said prophecies, such as Daniel's vision in chapters 10-12, will be

---

99 Paul Lederach, *Third Way*, 31.

realized in the future. This is highly problematic for a proper Christology, a biblical view of Jesus, in that it lessens the importance of Jesus in the climax of the biblical narrative. Sam Storms explained:

> The central and controlling thesis that I believe is warranted by the biblical text is that the fulfillment of Israel's prophetic hope as portrayed in the Old Testament documents is found in the person and work of Jesus Christ and the believing remnant, the church, which he established at his first coming. The point is that Jesus Christ and his Church are the focal and determining point of all prophecy.[100]

Every OT feast, holiday, celebration, or institution—including the Sabbath, the Temple, and all the sacrifices—find their fulfillment in Jesus Christ. They were in their original intention an imperfect foreshadow of what Jesus would fulfill in entirety in himself. To even suggest as dispensationalists do that some OT prophecy has not met its fulfillment in Jesus is an outright denial that Jesus was and is sufficient in his life, death, and resurrection to accomplish all that the Father had set out for him to do.[101]

Even though Jesus declares that the Old Testament finds complete fulfillment in himself, dispensationalists tend to skip over the life of Jesus, the ethics of Jesus in the Sermon on the Mount, and the reality of the kingdom in the works of Jesus.

Seeking a Better Hermeneutic: "Where one begins in Bible interpretation influences the way the kingdom is understood."[102] We have begun our response to rapture theology with the Anabaptist understanding of the kingdom of God from a biblical foundation. If one begins with a point of reference outside of the Bible, with an invented idea of late and unprecedented origins, then one may see "rapture" in the text in question.

Many biblical references in rapture theology could be unpacked and debunked, but we will look at "rapture" itself in 1 Thessalonians 4:17. Darby and others cannot be faulted too heavily for misusing the term in this text: "Then we who are alive, who are left, will be caught up together with them (the resurrected saints) in the clouds to meet the Lord in the air, and so we will be with the Lord always." Most readers of this verse get caught up with the term "caught up" and quickly relate the expression to pretribulational rapture.

---
100 Sam Storms, 16.
101 Sam Storms, 25.
102 Paul Lederach, 26.

Many details need to be addressed in this text. Of first importance is acknowledging that Paul was not teaching an eschatological lesson in 1 Thessalonians 4:13-18 but a pastoral one. "Therefore encourage one another with these words" provides the pastoral encouragement to a congregation that had anxiety about the followers of Jesus who had already died. So the main question Paul addressed had to do with those who believed in Jesus but had died before Jesus returned: Will they be at a disadvantage at the second coming of Christ?

The answer Paul provided was assuring: The dead in Christ will be raised first. Then those believers still alive will be "caught up," an expression translated from the Greek *harpazo*, which means "to seize, snatch away, or take by force." Paul's primary message to the congregation soothes their fears that the dead in Christ are not forgotten but will have a front-row view of the *parousia*, the coming of Christ.

Christ's second coming in this text begs explanation. Darby, Lindsey, and others failed to understand the nature of the *parousia*. The term refers to an official divine or imperial visit, the coming of a god or king to a city.[103] These events were cause for a great celebration with all the pomp and ceremony appropriate for a celebrity of this magnitude. If a person of global importance were to visit a small agrarian town on his world tour, it would make headlines and could not be kept quiet. Thus, the *parousia* could not be a secret event. In fact, Paul writes, "For the Lord himself will descend from heaven with a cry of command, with the voice of an archangel, and with the sound of the trumpet of God." (16). In contrast to Darby's "secret rapture," the archangel's call and the trumpet of God are *not secret*. If the *parousia* were a secret event, why is the coming of Jesus met with such fanfare?

What happens next in the text changes the preconceived notions of popular eschatology if read honestly. Those who are alive will be caught up with the dead in Christ to "meet" the Lord in the air. "To meet the Lord in the air…" is a technical term describing the custom of sending a delegation outside of the city to receive a person of importance who was approaching the town.[104] There are two examples of this expression in the New Testament: 1) When Jesus came to Jerusalem, the so-called triumphal entry in John 12:13 and the people who had come to the feast took palm branches to meet him; 2) When Paul came to Rome, "And the brothers there, when they heard about us, came as far as the Forum of Appius and Three Taverns to meet us" (Acts 28:15).

Reading the text in this manner changes the outcome. Christians will not be whisked away (leaving their clothes behind as in the Left Behind scenario)

---

103 J. Richard Middleton, *A New Heaven and a New Earth* (Grand Rapids, MI: Baker Academic, 2014), 223.
104 Ibid, 223.

to heaven but will return with Jesus to the earth. As J. Richard Middleton describes it,

> Since cemeteries were located outside city walls in the first century, often lining the main road leading to the city, Paul's readers could vividly imagine the scenario of the dead in Christ being raised as the king passed by, before those in the city went out to meet him as he approached the city gates. This also makes sense Paul's statement that 'God will bring with him [Christ] those who have died' (1 Thess. 4:14); this suggests that those raised from the graves, who have met the returning Lord, will then enter the city with him.[105]

Where rapture theology takes believers out of the world prior to the tribulation, this reading places believers dead and living at the end of time when Christ comes to claim his realm as King. We would have to conclude that the text is not about the removal of believers from the world at all.

Summarizing Anabaptist Objections to Rapture Theology: If the point has not been made clear up to this point, rapture theology is not compatible with the Anabaptist understanding of the Bible. The core values and biblical ethics of being followers of Christ would be circumvented if Anabaptists continue to pursue dispensational theology. To summarize, here are a few key objections Anabaptists have regarding rapture theology and why it needs to be "left behind."

a) Rapture theology tends to read the Bible from an ego-temporal perspective. Hal Lindsey and those who come after him view the prophecies of Ezekiel, Daniel, and Revelation as if they were written directly to our times. A just and fair hermeneutic would read these books of the Bible in the proper context by first considering how the original audience received them.

b) Rapture theology fails to read the Bible honestly. Darby, Lindsey, LaHaye, and Jenkins possess an inconsistent methodology of reading the Bible. If the basic principle of evangelical interpretation of the Bible is a literal reading and interpretation, these writers fail to follow that principle. Daniel's vision contains a lion, a bear, a leopard, and a goat, but are they literal? Yet dispensational/rapture theology disregards the literal rule of interpretation by assigning meanings to the figures that were never intended nor possible. Another

---

105 Ibid, 224.

example of this inconsistency is found in Revelation 13, where the beasts are interpreted as representing future historical figures, whereas the number of the beast in the same chapters is interpreted literally.

c) Rapture theology breeds contempt for the ecology of the earth. The escapism of rapture theology creates a disregard for the state of the natural world because, as many evangelicals have quipped, "It's all going to burn up anyway." These comments do not take into account the future of the earth in God's plan, for as Paul said,

> For the creation was subjected to futility, not willingly, but because of him who subjected it, in hope that the creation itself will be set free from its bondage to corruption and obtain the freedom of the glory of the children of God. For we know that the whole creation has been groaning together in the pains of childbirth until now. (Romans 8:20-22)

Yet the Rapture adherent would say, "The earth is not to be conserved or cared for: it will go to hell along with history and every person or animal or thing on earth that is not a Christian."[106]

In an age of awareness concerning the state of the natural world, and as biblical scholars rediscover the biblical mandate given to God's people to be stewards of creation, rapture theology opposes both streams of earth-consciousness. This is the world God has given us, and we are here to take care of this gift. Marlin Jeschke wrote,

> The biblical message about a human community and a renewed earth is something that has been recovered after centuries of Hellenized Christian thought. The Christian faith does not speak about an escape to heaven; it does not speak about the abandonment of God's creation. From this perspective, one could wish that Lindsey had entitled his book *The New Great Planet Earth*.[107]

d) Rapture theology does not take seriously the exaltation of Jesus as Lord. If it did, it would acknowledge that the kingdom is not only in the future, but it is here. Based on the above discussion of what the kingdom means, Anabaptist thought takes seriously the exaltation of Jesus Christ as Lord. And in confessing his lordship, we recognize the presence of the kingdom of God with

---

106 Hal Lindsey, *The Rapture: Truth or Consequences* (New York: Bantam, 1983), esp. 210.
107 Kraus, *Evangelicalism and Anabaptism*, 138-139. Marlin Jeschke wrote a chapter in this volume entitled "Pop Eschatology: Hal Lindsey and Evangelical Theology."

Christ as King in the way we conduct our lives, our marriages, our families, and our business dealings.

e) Rapture theology, as expressed in the Left Behind series, ignores the life of Christ as exemplary for believers in the present life. In fact, the Left Behind series of novels promotes an ethic in the so-called thousand-year reign that permits a Christian to lie and to kill those who do not follow Christ. In an excellent survey and critique, Loren L. Johns summarizes the ethic of the millennial believer:

> They lie. They express their desire to hurt people—just the evil ones, of course (3:91). They kill enemies with their bare fists. Buck "drove his fist square into the young guard's nose with all he could muster. He felt the crush of cartilage, the cracking of teeth, and the ripping of flesh. The back of [the guard's] head hit the floor first" (4:347). Christians shoot at non-Christians, saying, "I'll kill you, you ___" (4:351). They seethe with anger (6:150, 282, 317, 387) and rage (4:400; 7:50), with the desire to kill (4:400) and to seek revenge (6:395; 7:50). There is even a subtle spiritual contest among the tribulation Force about who seethes with anger more: Chloe or Rayford or Hattie (5:256; cf. also 10:7), as if seething with anger were the most reliable fruit of the Spirit in the tribulation. They spew venom (5:300). Rayford hopes God lets him pull the trigger and murder Carpathia (4:416), as does Mac (12:51). Rayford wants to be "God's hit man" (5:100).[108]

Clearly, literature like this has theological and moral difficulties. Evangelicals who read the Bible and follow Christ cannot help but see the inconsistency with discipleship in the pages of the Left Behind literature.

f) Rapture theology disregards the suffering of believers in closed nations. Rapture theology tells us that the suffering of the world will get worse in the tribulation. That may find substance in the prophecies of the New Testament. However, the followers of Christ who live in closed countries where Christianity is illegal may argue that life as a believer could not get much worse. Many disciples of Jesus have died over several centuries, and the church would be remiss in ignoring that tribulation has already begun for believers the world over. These are the latter days that Jesus talked about; these are the days when the world expresses its hatred for Christians because of the name of Christ.

---

108 Loren L. Johns, "Conceiving Violence: The Apocalypse of John and the Left Behind Series," Direction: A Mennonite Brethren Forum, Fall 2005 · Vol. 34 No. 2, pp. 194–214.

Chapter Six:
Evangelicals, Anabaptists, and the Peace Challenge

The year was 1940-something, and my father was performing alternative service in Banff National Park. When conscripted to serve in the army to fight in Europe, dad claimed conscientious objector status before the judge. Alternative service for conscientious objectors consisted of a variety of work: forestry service in national parks, farm laborers, and other tasks that would support the nation in a non-combative manner. Dad was sent west to Banff for a little less than a year to help clear dead trees and perform other odd jobs.

One day, a fellow conscientious objector walked into a store in Banff only to be brusquely told to leave. The manager stated that he did not serve cowards or shirkers and that this man should take his business elsewhere. Dad saw a challenge. He walked into the same store and began looking around. Again, the manager challenged the newcomer: "What are you doing here? What do you want?" My father replied, "I work for the government and I'm here to get supplies." Convinced of the veracity of my father's reply, he let him alone. The government issue clothing the men wore likely did not betray their status, and dad used it to his advantage. His reply about being a government employee was confidently expressed to mollify the manager.

My father's experience reveals the ongoing attitude toward those who refuse to solve conflict with violence. Unpatriotic, cowardly, yellow, and weak are just a few of the terms thrown at those who object to the use of force to protect or defend oneself or one's country. Whatever the manager's religious beliefs, he represents a typical evangelical response to the nonviolent option.

One aspect of the Anabaptist tradition evangelicals struggle with is the peace position. The peace position, or nonresistance as it is commonly known among Anabaptists, denotes the faith and life of those who believe that following Christ entails renouncing warfare and other violent means for gaining a particular goal. We can find the biblical basis for "nonresistance" in the words of Jesus who said, "Do not resist the one who is evil" (Matthew 5:39). Another common term used by Anabaptists is "pacifism," which comes from Jesus' words also, "Blessed are the peacemakers (Matthew 5:9). However, pacifism can be employed by other groups committed to nonviolence, just as nonresistance can, so we must distinguish these terms by prefacing them with "Christian."

Evangelicals and Anabaptists are both committed to reading the Bible faithfully and to following Jesus conscientiously. Even so, evangelicals tend not to see what Anabaptists see in the exemplary life of Christ: a nonviolent template to base one's life upon. Oddly enough, Anabaptists also struggle with their own interpretation of the life of Jesus when it comes to their commitment to nonviolence. Despite the example of Jesus in the Gospels, both traditions have had a hard time with nonresistance in the face of evil for different reasons.

Evangelical Resistance to Nonresistance

Evangelical hermeneutics is an invaluable model for reading and interpreting the Bible. We have learned a great deal about excellent biblical scholarship through many evangelical professors, writers, and pastors. For these passionate people of the Word to dismiss the biblical case for nonresistance suggests that their study has not culminated in the logical conclusion that careful examination would produce.

David Cramer proposes that evangelicals find the peace position to be incompatible with a faithful reading of Scripture.[109] A starting point for this reading finds its base in the Reformation principle of Sola scriptura, or "Scripture Alone," out of which comes a primary evangelical doctrine of sola fide, or "faith alone." If the foundation of Reformed doctrines—faith alone, Scripture alone, etc.—are to be held, a pacifist stance cannot be maintained, say evangelicals.[110] If pacifism becomes an expectation of Christians, Christians will become legalistic in their attempts to uphold pacifism. In other words, peacemaking and nonviolence as a standard of the Christian faith will lead believers to conclude that they are righteous by virtue of their pacifism. They will empty the stand of "by faith alone" as a means of coming to God and being saved by the work of God.

Hermeneutics aside, evangelicals in North America have been steeped in the ideology of the "Christian Nation," an issue discussed earlier in this volume. It bears repeating that when an institution of a nation, like the United States Marine Corps, bears the motto "God—Country—Corps," and the

---

109 Burkholder and Cramer, *The Activist Impulse*, "Evangelical Hermeneutics, Anabaptist Ethics," by David S. Cramer, 381.
110 The five solas of the Reformation are sola scriptura (by Scripture alone), sola fide (by faith alone), sola gratia (by grace alone), solus Christus or solo Christo ("Christ alone" or "through Christ alone"), and soli Deo gloria.

currency likewise bears the slogan "In God We Trust," a tight relationship is expressed concerning what the average American considers Christian. If the evangelical believes his or her nation is ordained by God to be a "city on a hill," a testimony to the world of what a godly nation looks like, then the defense of that nation will be a high priority. It has been said by some observers that US soldiers who embark on a tour of duty are prayed for in evangelical churches as if they were missionaries heading out into the world to proclaim a gospel. In their view, these soldiers are embarking on a "holy crusade" to protect American values (read "Christian") from foreign hostile forces. When it appears that the "enemy" exists within the borders of America, preserving the "Christian nation" takes other forms. With this type of perspective, it is easy to see why evangelicals philosophically consider pacifism an obstacle to the glory of God as they perceive it.

The peace position Anabaptists advocate also may appear to be a stumbling block to the justice system. If retributive violence was discarded, capital punishment abolished, and judicial sentencing and prison reform overhauled, a widespread fear of murderers and rapists running free would engulf the nation. Would there be justice for the families of the victims of sexual assault and homicide? Would there be satisfaction, a just punishment, for the crimes committed? Evangelicals would typically say no. Owing to the entrenched penal substitution atonement theology and the popular position of eternal conscious torment regarding hell, many evangelicals would be pro-capital punishment. It is simply unbiblical for some evangelicals to allow convicted persons to be shown mercy since they showed none to their victims. The punishment fits the crime.

Anabaptist Resistance to Nonresistance

Anabaptists and Mennonites who have grown up in North America have been inundated with the themes of patriotism through movies, songs, and novels all their lives. The myth of redemptive violence dominates the cultural landscape of America to the extent that the only solution to hostility is a reciprocal attitude and behavior.[111] Anabaptist resistance to nonresistance continues from generation to generation as each cohort of young adults has to grapple again with the ethics of war and violence.

Every time a new war erupts, young adults renew the conversation concerning the conflict between duty to country and obedience to Christ and

---

111 See "The Myth of Redemptive Violence," by Walter Wink, https://www2.goshen.edu/~joannab/women/wink99.pdf

whether the two are incompatible. At different times in Europe, the Napoleonic Wars (1803-1815) or the Crimean War (1853-1856)—to name two that affected Anabaptists—Mennonites were forced to contribute with food stuffs or with direct involvement, both of which were a dilemma for a people who did not support war in any form. In the US, American Mennonites faced conscription for the first time during the Civil War (1861-1865) when young men were drafted by Confederate forces to defend the Southern way of life (i.e., the institution of slavery). Anabaptist churches were not prepared to answer these challenges biblically or theologically, and many young men ended up in uniform. Some put on the uniform and picked up the gun by choice; others did so against their consciences.

With the advent of World War I, both Canadian and American Mennonites were again faced with the question of patriotic duty or conscientious objection. In this case and again in World War II, more and more young adults of Mennonite background purposely chose to go and fight. Within the gaps between wars, the church did little to prepare these young adults to wrestle with the choice of nonviolence in the face of war and hostility. With each military action, the general conviction seemed to lessen.

Resistance to nonresistance within the Anabaptist churches has never been higher than it is in the twenty-first century. Different polls will tell different stories, but in straw polls conducted unofficially, the commitment to nonviolence among Mennonites is roughly split down the middle.

Why do Mennonites/Anabaptists today regard violence as a valid option for handling specific conflicts? First, personal defense has always been an issue. The age-old question, "What would you do if someone broke into your house and threatened your family?" has never gone away. And most husbands would answer that they would fight to protect their wives and children. Second, with the threat of terrorist attacks—when a plane is hijacked for nefarious ends, or domestic attacks—when a crazed gunman walks into a movie theater and opens up on the audience, a nonviolent approach seems impotent for the situation. Third, as has been mentioned, culture teaches us that a real man fights, exacts revenge, and finds justice through redemptive violence. Anabaptist young people have bought into this culture of gun-law through almost no fault of their own.

Biblical Foundations of the Peace Position

Are evangelicals correct in their hermeneutical understanding of the peace position? Is it in conflict with sola scriptura? Are Anabaptists abandoning a key element of their faith perspective and accepting the status quo? Do biblical foundations exist for the peace position that are both hermeneutically sound and ethically true?

We have discussed the Anabaptist approach to Scripture as being a straightforward hermeneutic. In conjunction with this approach, we have also recognized that when Jesus teaches an ethic or gives a command, Anabaptists take this teaching or command literally. In other words, they do not apply the teaching to a future millennium but regard the teaching as pertinent for living holy lives in the here and now. When discussing the biblical foundations of the peace position, we will present the teaching of Jesus in this light.

Matthew 5:38-42 – Do Not Resist an Evil Person: Beginning with the Sermon on the Mount, we find one of the most difficult passages to handle in terms of the peace position. It is not difficult to understand; it is difficult because we have a hard time embracing the principle in our contexts. Jesus said,

> You have heard that it was said, "An eye for an eye and a tooth for a tooth." But I say to you, **Do not resist** the one who is evil. But if anyone slaps you on the right cheek, turn to him the other also. And if anyone would sue you and take your tunic, let him have your cloak as well. And if anyone forces you to go one mile, go with him two miles. Give to the one who begs from you, and do not refuse the one who would borrow from you. (Matthew 5:38-42)

As mentioned previously, this text is the classic foundation for nonresistance in the Anabaptist tradition. Evangelical scholar, John Stott, called this "the highest point of the Sermon on the Mount, for which it is both most admired and most resented."[112] Indeed, the call to totally love one who intends or does evil to us is high and seemingly out of our reach. In the enactment of this love, we see a counter-cultural approach to the predominant theme in the North American culture of vengeance and redemptive violence.

What Jesus implied as well-known among his listeners was a quote from the Mosaic law. From Exodus 20, we observe the Ten Commandments, a summary of the moral law that Israel was to follow. Then in Exodus 21 to 23, we read the applications of this law on the life of Israel and its citizens, including case law regarding an injury to person and property. Jesus' reference to "an eye for an eye," found in this context, is but the tip of the iceberg: "But if

---

112 John R.W. Stott, *The Message of the Sermon on the Mount*, TBST (Downers Grove, IL: Inter-Varsity Press, 1978), 103.

there is harm, then you shall pay life for life, eye for eye, tooth for tooth, hand for hand, foot for foot, burn for burn, wound for wound, stripe for stripe" (Exodus 21:23-24). The Law's intention was to *limit* the compensation one might be owed in an injurious situation. "It thus had the double effect of defining justice and restraining revenge."113 Circumventing the courts, the Jews used this Mosaic prescription as an excuse to exact personal revenge, which it was originally meant to prevent.

Jesus said, "do not resist" the evil person; instead of revenge, offer a peculiar response. He gives four illustrations demonstrating how far the follower of Christ should go in expressing a love response to an evil action: when someone strikes you on the face; when someone sues you for your property; when someone presses you into service; and when someone begs for money. Jesus specifically instructs his followers when hit in the face to brace for another. He instructs his followers not to resist a legal prosecution. And when a soldier asks you to carry his bags for a mile, go an extra mile.[114] Finally, give to the one who asks for money. We must remember that these were only examples and that we are by no means limited by the four categories. When facing one with evil intentions, we must go all out in showing a loving response.

The implications of Matthew 5:39 are quite straightforward. When a person clearly has evil designs, we should not categorize them as an enemy. When they act out their evil intentions, be it physical or otherwise, we should not retaliate but respond according to the needs of the offending person. Even if such a response of love and nonretaliation makes no impact on the offender, their non-response is irrelevant since love does not depend on reciprocity. And finally, acting according to Matthew 5:39 may cost you in some way.[115]

Dietrich Bonhoeffer commented on this text saying,

> The only way to overcome evil is to let it run itself to a standstill because it does not find the resistance it is looking for. Resistance merely creates further evil and adds fuel to the flames. But when evil meets no opposition and encounters no obstacle but only patience endurance, its sting is drawn, and at last it meets an opponent which is more than its match. Of course, this can only happen when the last

---

113 Ibid, 104.
114 In the Ancient Near East, there was a custom/expectation that Roman soldiers could press a civilian into service to carry his military baggage for at least a mile. This was an obligation no one could refuse. Jesus used the custom as an example of offering extra service so that it applies not only to carrying military baggage but assisting anyone who demands it and then doubling it out of love.
115 Ronald J. Sider, *Brethren in Christ History & Life*, "An Anabaptist Perspective," 28 no 2 Aug 2005, 255-278, 264.

> ounce of resistance is abandoned, and the renunciation of revenge is complete. Then evil cannot find its mark, it can breed no further evil, and is left barren.[116]

Violence breeds more violence. The cycle is neverending because revenge is never satisfied. A classic example that lasted over a century was the Hatfield-McCoy feud beginning in the 1800s. Just when one party feels vindicated, the other party, feeling empty and violated, must restore their honor. And on it goes. Bonhoeffer was right in saying that the only response to evil is non-resistance.

Jesus himself provided the ultimate example of a nonviolent response to evil and claimed a resounding victory through it. Jesus called his disciples to this response because he suffered for them, leaving them this example to follow in his steps. He did not retaliate when insulted or beaten by his enemies but trusted in the One who is the supreme judge of all things (1 Peter 2:21-23). Bonhoeffer called this imitation of Christ's suffering the disciples' "visible participation" in the cross.[117]

Matthew 5:43-48 – Love Your Enemies: Jesus continued to shake the established manner of thinking about those who do evil by commanding his followers to love their enemies.

> You have heard that it was said, "You shall love your neighbor and hate your enemy." But I say to you, Love your enemies and pray for those who persecute you, so that you may be sons of your Father who is in heaven. For he makes his sun rise on the evil and on the good, and sends rain on the just and on the unjust. For if you love those who love you, what reward do you have? Do not even the tax collectors do the same? And if you greet only your brothers,[b] what more are you doing than others? Do not even the Gentiles do the same? You therefore must be perfect, as your heavenly Father is perfect.

The Mosaic law was specific in commanding the Israelite to love "the sons of your own people," giving Jews cause to live at peace with other Jews. Further, Moses taught the Israelites to "love your neighbor as yourself."[118] To the Jewish mind, "your neighbor" was a fellow Jew; anyone outside the Israelite race was an enemy. Jesus turned this thinking on its head when a lawyer put

---

116 Dietrich Bonhoeffer, *The Cost of Discipleship* (New York: Macmillan, 1968), 157-158.
117 Ibid, 161.
118 Leviticus 19:18

him to the test asking, "And who is my neighbor?" to which Jesus responded with the story of the Good Samaritan.[119] Suddenly, "my neighbor" is no longer my kinfolk or those of my race; my neighbor, according to the teaching of Jesus, is one who would naturally be my enemy.

Now Stott, the evangelical scholar, makes a caveat for how one is to understand the Old Testament hostility toward idolatrous and immoral people. He cited the observation that certain psalmists, like the author of Psalm 139:19-24, penned imprecatory psalms like this apart from personal animosity, but as a representative of God. The enemies of God are his own enemies; because he loves God, he hates those who oppose God. Stott writes,

> The truth is that evil men should be the object simultaneously of our 'love' and of our 'hatred,' as they are simultaneously the objects of God's... To 'love' them is ardently to desire that they will repent and believe, and so be saved. To 'hate' them is to desire with equal ardor that, if they stubbornly refuse to repent and believe, they will incur God's judgment.[120]

With great respect for Stott, we must object to such an interpretation that we are to hate those who refuse to believe as being an aberration of what Jesus just said in the Sermon on the Mount. The Apostle Paul clearly wrote that "while we were still weak, at the right time Christ died for the ungodly... For if while we were enemies we were reconciled to God by the death of his Son, much more, now that we are reconciled, shall we be saved by his life" (Romans 5:6, 10). Followers of Christ are implored to imitate the example of Christ who, while hanging on a tree, cried, "Father, forgive them..." and died for humankind while "we were enemies" of his person. If we have enemies, they are those who bear some hostility against us for bearing the name of Jesus and living a counter-culture lifestyle. These are the ones we are called to love. A believer cannot have enemies whom we gleefully categorize as such. "By our enemies Jesus means those who are quite intractable and utterly unresponsive to our love, who forgive us nothing when we forgive them all, who requite our love with hatred and our service with derision."[121] Bonhoeffer, another evangelical Lutheran writer, stated that Christian love draws no distinction between one enemy and another, except that some need more loving. What we would do for our brother by way of sacrifice, honor, and life, whom we love, we are also to do for our enemy, he says.

---

119 Luke 10:25-37
120 John Stott, *Sermon on the Mount*, 117.
121 Dietrich Bonhoeffer, *The Cost of Discipleship*, 164.

If we take Jesus' words to heart, we must abandon all excuses to avoid loving our enemy. Our enemy's life becomes more important to us than our own life, just as Christ regarded his own life forfeit for the sake of ours. If only our enemy, through our life—perhaps even our death—might see the love of God for him or her expressed in the complete pouring out of our own lives for their sakes. Taking Christ's words in this manner is not merely an Anabaptist reading; it follows the evangelical hermeneutic of getting into and under the text and unpacking its meaning so we might apply it to life.

Daniel 5 – The Handwriting on the Wall: From the Old Testament, we find a narrative in the book of Daniel where King Belshazzar has been partying using the vessels from Yahweh's temple as drinking cups. It is a serious case of blasphemy against the LORD and a mysterious hand begins to write words of judgment on the wall. The narrative is familiar, but our concern in this unit is the response of an evangelical Bible scholar who comments on this piece.

Tremper Longman III wrote an informative commentary on Daniel 5, specifically on the judgment of king Belshazzar for his blasphemy of the Lord, saying:

> Such an understanding intensifies the concept of blasphemy. Blasphemy is not just defacing a church or a cross. It is a misuse of any part of God's creation. An assault against a fellow human being is an act of blasphemy. After all, we are all created in the image of God (Gen. 1:27; James 3:9). An angry word spoken against a fellow believer is an act of blasphemy. After all, Christians are all temples of the Holy Spirit (1 Cor. 3:16). The destruction of the environment for selfish purposes is an act of blasphemy. The land, the air, the sea are each the creation of our holy God.[122]

What grabs our attention in this quote is the outcome of the logic used in explaining this narrative. With this evangelical interpretation of Daniel's narrative, would not the natural response of the Christian to war and violence be a position of peace and nonviolence? Yet while coming very close to saying so, Longman does not make that conclusion outright. The person created in

---

122 Tremper Longman III, *Daniel: The NIV Application Commentary* (Grand Rapids, MI: Zondervan, 1999), 152.

the image of God must not be destroyed since that person is more of a representative of God than any article from a cultic ritual. Furthermore, Longman writes that the earth itself is a gift from God that humankind has been authorized to be a steward of for the Lord's purposes. In summary, Longman's commentary on the narrative should conclude with a call to a nonresistance position regarding violence to a fellow human being.

Matthew 26:52-56 – No Need for Swords: Jesus exemplified his own stance regarding those who counted themselves his enemies when he was arrested in the Garden of Gethsemane. One of his disciples struck a servant of the priest on the ear, cutting it off. We can assume he was aiming for the servant's head and missed. Nevertheless, Jesus was perturbed at this show of violence on his behalf. He said to the disciple, "Put your sword back in its place. For all who take the sword will perish by the sword. Do you think that I cannot appeal to my Father, and he will at once send me more than twelve legions of angels?" (Matthew 26:52-53). But Jesus had not come to demonstrate his power and authority on the earth through force.

Exerting our own power, if we have any, by use of violence does not express the kingdom of God either. When a sword is flashed or a gun is fired with the intent of injuring or killing, can anyone truly say there is no anger in the effort? What goal will be accomplished in furthering the kingdom by violence?

Christian Nonresistance

Nonresistance is more than a conscientious objection to war or a refusal to engage in military service. The above examples of Christ's teaching and life reveal that the doctrine of nonresistance is a lifestyle founded on the way of love and the cross. Jesus was betrayed, insulted, reviled, scourged, and subjected to a slow, painful death by his enemies and yet did not retaliate. His purpose in redeeming humankind from the shackles of sin that had bound us since the Garden of Eden could only be accomplished by submitting to the violence of his enemies.

Evangelicals may retort that Christ's sacrifice was part of the plan of redemption and that his nonviolence was not an example to be followed. We cannot stand in his place and redeem anyone by holding to a peace position. True. However, as God through Christ reconciled us to himself, God then entrusted to us the ministry of reconciliation and continues to make his appeal to humankind through us.[123] Since God withheld his righteous wrath from humankind in order to make his love known, the Christian disciple does not repay evil for evil so that the love of God may be known through us.

The way of love and the cross lived by Christ, which eventually resulted in his death on the cross. Living according to the doctrine of nonresistance means the Christian disciple enters into the same experience with Christ. We crucify the self on the cross with Christ, follow his lead, and forgive as he forgave, knowing that people do not know what they are doing. Menno Simons, one of the founders of the Anabaptist movement in the sixteenth century, said:

> True Christians do not know vengeance, no matter how they are mistreated. In patience they possess their souls. Luke 21:18. And they do not break their peace, even if they should be tempted by bondage, torture, poverty, and besides, by the sword and fire. They do not cry, Vengeance, vengeance, as does the world; but with Christ they supplicate and pray: Father, forgive them; for they know not what they do. Luke 23:34; Acts 7:60.
>
> According to the declaration of the prophets, they have beaten their swords into plowshares and their spears into pruning hooks. They shall sit every man under his vine and under his fig-tree, Christ; neither shall they learn war anymore. Isa 2:4; Mic. 4:3.[124]

Conrad Grebel, a Swiss founder of Anabaptism, said that believing Christians are like sheep among wolves. Grebel taught that believers only reach their goal of eternal rest with God, not by fighting human beings with the sword, but by battling spiritual enemies with faith in Christ. Taking human life is outside the realm of the Christian since we are no longer under the old covenant. As Paul wrote to the Ephesians, our battle in this life is not against flesh and blood, but against the dark powers of this fallen world (Ephesians 6:12). And our weapons are not of the usual type—as elsewhere Paul wrote that we fight with spiritual weapons that have a greater power of the divine variety to demolish more than brick-and-mortar walls—but arguments and deceptive philosophies that oppose the knowledge of God (2 Corinthians 10:3-6).

---

123 2 Corinthians 5:11-21
124 Menno Simons, *The Complete Writings of Menno Simons* (Scottdale, PA: Herald Press, 1984), 555.

A Cautious Digression

Just as the Anabaptist perspective advocates strongly for the peace position based on the life of Christ as portrayed in Scripture, I must add a word of caution to the promotion of this position. The argument "What would you do if someone broke into your home and threatened your family?" has been tediously regurgitated every time nonresistance is mentioned, but it demands attention.

Often, there emerges a hybrid response from Anabaptists who have drifted from the primary position of "peace at all costs," whereby they advocate peace on a global scale but confess that no one ought to mess with their family. The question for twenty-first-century Anabaptists and evangelicals is "Where is the line?" When and where does the line of our tolerance end and a reasonable defensive response begin?

The answer to those questions can only be speculative since one does not really know what options are available to that person in a violent situation and what response is actually possible. Nor do we know whether a person would have the volition to carry out the defensive action or the power to enact it.

These questions emphasize a need for reasonable thought regarding the historic peace position in light of the reality of violence in our world. Anabaptists tend to maintain a black-and-white view of violence that leads to an inability to process violent instances in current events and media. As a result, Anabaptists tend to have blinders over their eyes when it comes to actual violence. Much thought on violence centers on hypothetical situations and speculation in Anabaptist circles since most of us do not face the threat of persecution.

Violence and violent occurrences are much more complicated than the media portrays in their quick sound bites. A news story of a murder-suicide on an internet news feed provides a snapshot of the key events but provides very little in motivation or the psychological conditioning of the person in question. Yet the comments section fills quickly with the judgments of many readers who presume to know the mind of the killer. A mother takes the life of her young child and then kills herself—which is the greater tragedy, the mother's violence toward herself or toward her innocent child? Judgment falls on the mother because she had a choice; the child had no choice at all. Yet modern psychology may tell us that freedom of choice might not be as free as we are led to believe. However, we do not know what forces and influences caused this mother to make the choices she did. Personality traits, traumatic childhood experiences, mental health issues, and the twists and turns of the woman's life are all unknown to us. We do not excuse the violence, but perhaps we can understand the background a little and thus garner compassion for the aggressor as well as the victim.[125]

Presuming that evangelicals of a Calvinist nature are weighing in on this conversation, the doctrine of predestination presents a different perspective, albeit not a satisfying one. With predestination comes the answer to this unexplainable and mysterious force behind our actions—we cannot help ourselves. Freedom to choose is lost since we are destined to do what we do. The mother thus could not help herself but was predestined to kill her child. We cannot land on that logic as being a reasonable answer to the violence of this situation.

James Reimer uses the metaphor of a Scrabble game to explain the paradox of freedom and destiny. With a jigsaw puzzle, the shape of the finished product is predetermined, much like predestination in the Calvinist perspective. However, a Scrabble game involves a complex combination of factors determined by the rules of the game, such as luck, skill, intelligence, memory, and interaction. How the game will conclude is not obvious as you play each round. When the game does conclude, you can see in hindsight where it was headed. Those who do not believe in God call this fate; believers perceive that divine power was at work in which humans participate. Evangelical Calvinists tend to have a rigid view of how the pieces come together, seeing that they are foreordained. Anabaptists, by contrast, tend to lean toward a freedom of choice to act lovingly or nonviolently in a world of evil. The former finds the root of violence within the divine plan and seems fine with God's purpose in violence. The latter does not accept that God ordains violence but cannot seem to get to the heart of violence or its irrationality. For the Anabaptist, there is no easy answer, but that should be the saving grace of that position. Painting each encounter of violence with the same wide brush does not provide comfort or grace to those involved.

Central to the Anabaptist understanding of the gospel is the primary authority of the Bible for all faith and action. When the two conflict, Anabaptists have trouble processing the issues. In particular, reconciling the stories of violence, even where God appears to have sanctioned the violence in the Old and New Testaments, with Anabaptist convictions about the nonviolence of Jesus has been a difficult journey for Anabaptists. Scholars have at times accused Anabaptists of being Marcionites for the way they separate the Old Testament God of violence from the New Testament Jesus who brings peace. When Anabaptist preachers focus more on the Gospels and Paul in their sermons, ignoring the Old Testament, the accusation finds some valid-

---

125 This "Digression" unit is based upon the writings of James Reimer in his book *Mennonites and Classical Theology* (Kitchener, ON: Pandora Press, 2001), 488-492.

ity. Ultimately, Anabaptists have a challenging time dealing with a God who judges, punishes, kills, and orders his people to conquer nations by the sword.

What is violence? We tend to define it in physical terms where injuries to the flesh are experienced. However, Reimer cites the instances where Anabaptists have used the ban to remove people from the membership and fellowship of the church as a form of psychological and social violence.[126] Anabaptists may not use the sword, but there are other ways to damage the psyche of a person apart from physical violence. Excluding persons from the fellowship of believers often did more damage to the faith of the banned person than return them to fellowship. Anabaptists envisioned themselves as peaceful people, yet they had some skeletons in the closet when it came to church discipline.

Having turned over the rocks on the people who esteem the doctrine of nonviolence, we must remember that the biblical foundations of this doctrine continue to teach a position of peace based on the life of Christ. Even if the people get it wrong, that does not make the perspective erroneous. It does mean that as people called by Christ's name, we must continue to process the real-world issues of violence, both physical and psychological, from the perspective of being a nonviolent people.

---

126 "The Ban," also known as excommunication, was used by Anabaptist congregations as a form of church discipline. When a member of the fellowship was discovered to be involved in sinful activity, that person was implored to repent according to Matthew 18:15-17. If repentance was not forthcoming, the fellowship of believers would bar that person from worship, fellowship, and even social functions outside of the congregation (within the community where that person lived). Even within the home, a spouse was to have as little to do with the sinning person as possible. The goal of this treatment was to bring the person to repentance and hopefully to reconcile with the church. This did not happen as often as envisioned.

Chapter Seven:
Evangelism — When We Go Fishing

I am not a fisherman.

The prospect of hooking a fish and then having to touch its slimy body to withdraw my hook is not appealing to me. Thoughts of eating fish do not make me salivate. I can live without fishing or eating fish.

Ironically, I was placed in the fishing skill at Bible camp when I counseled for two summers ~~at a popular camp~~ in my teen years. Apparently, I was not skilled enough for archery or canoeing, so I kept being dumped in the fishing skill. One perk of this predicament was that I had the responsibility of driving the fishing boat. I would take the campers out on a boat trip and teach them about trolling. If I am honest about these expeditions, I drove the boat just fast enough so that the lures would bounce along the surface of the water where the fish could not bite them. If a fish was caught, the campers became squeamish and I had to dehook the fish.

When Jesus called the first disciples, he invited them to go fishing. "Follow me, and I will make you fishers of men" (Matthew 4:19). Being more of a horse-and-rope guy, I would have been more intrigued if Jesus had said, "Saddle up, and I will teach you how to lasso some souls for the kingdom." But he didn't, and Jesus wasn't talking about "hooking" men and women with bait. The imagery of casting a net has a very different nuance.

Fishing for men and women as a metaphor for the relationship Jesus would have with his disciples was a natural one to choose. It appealed to the men where they were in life, even if the meaning was not fleshed out for the reader of the Gospel. A similar metaphor was used in Jeremiah 16:16, where the Lord declares, "Behold, I am sending for many fishers..." who will catch his people. However, the context in Jeremiah is judgment and they are being caught in order to be punished, a punishment they will not escape. And to be quite clear, it is no thrill for the fish to be caught. Fishing for men and women, in the context of good news, in order to catch and slaughter them, does not fit the meaning Jesus gives to this invitation.

When the net is cast out and the fish are brought into the boat or onto shore, we cannot help but see an element of judgment in the event. The act of fishing divides the caught from the uncaught, just as there will be a sorting of the wheat and the weeds in the kingdom of God. Some are in and some are out. To call out these men to learn the art of fishing for people invites these disciples to proclaim "good news" and to rescue people from rather than catch them for judgment.[127] This kind of fishing casts a wide net for the sake of bringing many sons and daughters into the kingdom of God, into the Father's family.

A few implications can be made from Jesus' fishing metaphor:

Fishing for the kingdom is not an activity one does alone; teams are established. Peter, James, John, and Andrew fished as families and in partnership with other fishermen from the community. When Jesus sends out the disciples on "training exercises," he sends them out in twos at the very least (Luke 10:1). And when Paul embarked on his missionary endeavors, he took various people with him as team members, including Barnabas, John Mark, Timothy, Silas, and others. Evangelism ought not to be done as a solo effort.

Fishing for the kingdom involves following after Jesus. He invited the fishermen to be with him, learning from and modeling their lives on his life. The gospel accounts reveal a Jesus who showed compassion on the sick, patience with the slow-to-grasp-truth (disciples, crowds, etc.), and courage in confrontation with the establishment. Jesus was not arrogant, did not pressure the unbelieving (the rich young ruler), and did not consider numbers over genuine faith. When crowds were following him because of his popularity, he challenged them, "If anyone would come after me, let him deny himself and take up his cross and follow me" (Mark 8:34). That is not a catch-all statement, but a call to come and die.

Fishing for the kingdom will mean getting your hands dirty. As I attempted to avoid the slime of the fish, we cannot avoid the messiness of getting involved with unregenerated people. Sin is messy; people are messy for having chosen sin and sinfulness. But Jesus entered the mess of humanity as a human himself to dive right into the relationship that would rescue. He did not sin but did not hesitate to relate to those who sinned in order to redeem them from sin. That's messy work.

How evangelicals and Anabaptists envision the work of "fishing" differs in theology if not in practice. While the two are quite similar, some definite areas of concern need to be addressed if we are going to be evangelical and Anabaptist in our partnership with Jesus' work.

Evangelical Vision for Evangelism

Evangelicals are passionate about evangelism. At least, they give lip service to the ideal of winning "souls" for Jesus. That sounds harsh, but North American

---

127 R.T France, *The Gospel of Mark* (Grand Rapids, MI: Eerdman's, 2002), 96-97.

zeal for participating in evangelism ranks fairly low on the list of things a Christian really wants to do. Some even say that "evangelism" is a dirty word among evangelicals, churning up feelings of guilt rather than motivation. Yet it remains a core value of evangelical understanding regarding being the church.

Among North American evangelicals there remains a strong conviction that the proclamation of the gospel and its acceptance by the masses will transform society. Consequently, a society favoring the Christian worldview of government and politics will by this faith choose the moral high ground on matters of ethical, moral, and spiritual concern. If people accept the gospel of Jesus Christ, the natural outcome will be the progression toward a Christian society. According to the evangelical mindset, the goal of evangelism is to create a new world order, whereby the conversion of the powerful elite will benefit the poor and less fortunate. If the wealthy and powerful individuals become Christ-followers, the big-picture vision of an evangelized nation trickles down to the thumbnail level of society.

At the same time, evangelicalism maintains an individualistic perspective of evangelism and salvation. Evangelism appeals are made to the person, not persons, where they are in their journey. A prospective convert at a revival meeting will be addressed through the dynamic and heartfelt invitation of the speaker, possibly being made to feel guilty for sins and then relieved to hear that those sins are forgiven. The emotional roller coaster lands on the decision of the individual to accept the invitation to accept Christ. An evangelist's all-important objective is to "score" that decision for Jesus. There is then both a mass appeal and an individual invitation in evangelical evangelism.

Evangelical Foundations for Evangelism

At the heart of evangelical evangelism are four fundamental values that drive the movement forward.[128] As we discussed earlier, "evangelical" as a term is derived from the Greek word *euangelion,* from which we get the term "evangel." An evangel is one who proclaims the good news. To be "evangelical" assumes, then, that the person who identifies as such will be a herald of the good news of Jesus Christ crucified and risen from the dead. The four fundamental values are based on this understanding.

The first value centers on the belief that all spiritual truths can be found in the pages of the Bible. This is known as biblicism. Positively, being a person who depends on the Bible as the source of authority and knowledge is

---

[128] David Bebbington defined evangelicalism with these four perennial manifestations of the movement: Biblicism, Crucicentrism, Conversionism, and Activism. I have adapted them for this chapter.

known as a Biblicist. Negatively, a Biblicist may be seen as interpreting the Bible too literally and using the Bible to guide them through every situation. Regardless, of the negative aspersions, evangelicals have great respect for the authority of the Bible for faith and life.

Second, based on their high view of Scripture, evangelicals believe in the centrality of the doctrine of the cross or atonement. Only through the work of Christ on the cross can a person be saved from their sins.

Third, evangelicals believe that all human beings need to be converted through a transforming experience by faith in Jesus Christ. Often, this conversion is perceived as a dramatic event where the old life of sin gets "killed" and the new life in Christ begins. Testimonies of conversion entail reliving that moment when you were "born again" and everything in your life changed because of Jesus. Unfortunately for those who grew up in the church, their conversion story may not be all that dramatic; there will not be a "before" and "after" photo montage because the change was a gradual progression over several years. Conversionism, as evangelicals call it, casts feelings of doubt on our legitimacy regarding our conversion. Long-term conversion stories do not have the same appeal as the dramatic "lightning strike" conversions.

Fourth and finally, evangelicals value activism, where those who have experienced conversion manifest their joy of being saved by wanting others to know salvation as well. Due to the lack of drama in the long-term conversion stories of many who grew up in the evangelical church, activism has fallen off in contemporary evangelicalism.

Activism, the desire to see others saved and have a personal relationship with Jesus, may have declined in recent decades for several reasons. One reason may be that activism has been replaced as an evangelical identifier with orthodoxy. We tend to discern who the Christians really are by what they believe in terms of correct doctrine as opposed to their activity in reaching out to others. If our theological convictions are correct but do not lead us to share those convictions with others, are they really convictions? Believing that Jesus died for our sins may stir our hearts and bring us to God, but if that revelation of God's love for us truly moves us, then we will be unable to contain our joy.

Conversion stories themselves have contributed to a false understanding of evangelistic activism. Extreme examples of conversion tend to divide evangelicals into "haves" and "have nots." Not all of us can have a John Wesley experience of conversion where he literally felt a glowing in his chest. Wesley said, "I felt my heart strangely warmed, I felt I did trust in Christ, Christ alone for my salvation and an assurance was given me that he had taken away my sins." Wesley's experience created a paradigm shift in evangelicalism that advanced a new kind of personal faith and assurance. However, the intellectual aspect of conversion was weakened in favor of the emotional and relational elements of conversion. The subsequent evangelical awakenings in New England were a movement toward individual participation in a spiritual reality, which focused on a subjective choice. Some were inclined to see this as a work of man's choice; others believed that the "warming of the heart" was an act of God alone. But for those who come to Christ in a rational and non-emotional conversion, suspicions of genuineness arise from certain corners of evangelicalism.

Activism, the fourth leg of the evangelical table, wobbles in this generation for these and other reasons, which will be explored. Whatever the issues may be, for whatever reason we fear evangelism, activism is missing in our orthopraxy and we need to rediscover that zeal.

Revival: The Evangelical Watchword for Evangelism

Revival! When evangelicals assess the declining morality of the nation and the apostatizing of the church in relation to the ills of society, the cure-all for these "diseases" is revival. Signs of moral decay include the rise of LGBTQ rights, the legal triumphs of abortion rights activists, and the idol-worship of athletes and movie stars, many of whom have less than stellar private lives. If the church would return to its Christian origins and pray for revival with all earnestness, evangelicals believe that the clock can be turned back on the advancement of unbelief and paganism in North American culture.

Revival! Many of our seniors remember with fondness the golden era of revival when preachers would come and speak bluntly, albeit powerfully, about sin and sinners. With a great fiery and emotional appeal, scores of weeping folks would go forward at the invitation to accept Christ, confess their sins, and recite the sinner's prayer. Thousands were impacted by the crusades and tent meetings of the forties and fifties, their lives changed forever having found the missing piece of their faith. A new fervor enveloped the churches as they began to wake up to the necessity of evangelism. Those with a nostalgia for that golden era or those who yearn for a fresh wind to awaken the twenty-first-century church pine and pray for another revival like the ones of the past.

The problem with revival is that it is based on a faulty assumption that many North Americans already know the truth but have not activated it. Many of those folks who were revived in the forties and fifties were raised in a tradition of Christianity by their parents or were exposed to the gospel frequently by other means. They were revived because they simply needed to be awakened to what they already knew. However, the cold reality of our generation is that many people in North America do not know who Jesus Christ is, apart from a name used as profanity. Before people can be "revived" then, they must have been "vived" beforehand.[129]

When I pastored in an urban setting some years ago, I met a young man on the doorstep of our church building who exemplified this unrevived state. Standing in the shade of the entrance, he appeared to have been bicycling in the heat of the day. As I approached him, I said hello and asked if I could help him with anything. I had never seen him before. He immediately asked, "What is this place?" I was dumbfounded for a second *Is he kidding?* I thought. I told him it was a church building. "What do you do in there?" Again, an odd question. As the questions continued, it slowly dawned on me that this young man had never heard of Christ or Christians before. At the very least, Christianity had never been explained to him before.

While we might categorize this as an isolated experience, it is not. A colleague went to a popular riverside park and recreation area to talk with people about Jesus. He came across several individuals who claimed to know nothing of Jesus Christ when asked. One fellow said he had never even heard the name Jesus before my friend mentioned him. As the common vernacular declares, "His mind was blown." People do not automatically know who Jesus is when spoken of; therefore, how can there be revival?

Revival speaks to a Christian setting, not to a purely evangelistic setting where people have not heard of Christ. As Rodney Clapp wrote regarding revivalism,

> The most prominent American evangelistic paradigm from the eighteenth century right into our day—revivalism—is a profoundly Constantinian approach to Christian mission. The very designation implies a Constantinian context. Revivalism aims to revive or revitalize the pre-existing but now latent faith of birthright Christians. It presupposes a knowledge of the languages and practices of faith. It is an evangelistic strategy that depended on the American population being Protestant.[130]

Otherwise known as "Christianese," the "languages and practices of faith" are an unknown language to the seeker or pre-Christian, or unbeliever if you

---

129 "Vived" is a term I concocted to refer to the condition of being introduced to the gospel for the first time having never heard of Jesus beforehand. When a person has lived for the Lord and fallen away due to a variety of circumstances and, somehow, is reminded of the importance of faith in Christ, then they are revived.
130 Rodney Clapp, *A Peculiar People* (Downers Grove, IL: Inter-Varsity Press, 1996), 163.

will. We speak of "repentance," "salvation," "righteousness," and even "sin," expecting the uninitiated to know what we are talking about.

Revivalism as a paradigm for evangelism contains several deficiencies in this respect and is not an effective paradigm for this generation. True evangelism, in the New Testament sense, was not a matter of inviting people to remember what they knew. It was actually an event when the individual was invited to join a community of people who were embracing the new humanity that resulted from faith in Christ.[131] Revivalism, those tent meetings of the past, focused so intently on the individual decision that those who made the decision had no idea what to do next. There are many stories of "converts" who went to the altar once, then a few days, weeks, or years later would go forward again, unsure of whether the last "decision" took. It was as if a flagging faith needed a boost from another visit to the altar.

The message of revival conveys the idea that being born again is a very personal, very private experience that brings peace and healing to the inner being. Evangelists speak of the benefits the sinner will receive when they repent, but few speak of the costs of following Jesus. Those elements that are least marketable—self-sacrifice, servanthood, the way of the cross, identifying with the poor and lowly—are not talked about in the heat of the moment. Once we get them "in," we can talk about the nitty-gritty of expectation, let's just get them saved first. The emotional appeal to the individual and her present needs outweighs the rational processing of what it means to follow Jesus in the long term. Revival in this guise does not appeal to the growing number of educated and intellectual sojourners who actually want to know why they should follow Jesus apart from the emotional reasons.

With revival, personal responsibility as a Christian to be involved in evangelism decreases as churches look to specialists to do the evangelizing. Activism that drives to see others "saved" lessens as the individual evaluates himself or herself as unqualified to convert the lost. They just do not have the gifts or the words to speak about their faith. Revivalists exacerbated this perception because they believed an event had to be conducted a certain way for God to work. If the right elements were in place, God would be faithful and conversion would follow. With the success of the big-name evangelists—Dwight Moody, Billy Sunday, and Billy Graham—the evangelical understanding of evangelism was that charismatic preaching played a critical role in revival. This was not for the little guy.

This kind of evangelism seeks to get people "born again." That in itself is not problematic. It's problematic that conversion is not about transforming

---

131 Ibid, 165.

the individual alone but is an incorporation into the spiritual reality of the body of Christ. Salvation in isolation is not an option; when a woman or man declares faith in Christ and decides to live for Jesus, that person becomes part of the community of believers. Without this incorporation, the message of salvation trumps the church as an element of the gospel. Jesus never intended that the gospel and the church should so be separated.

Anabaptists and the Great Commission

When we think of the nineteenth and early twentieth-century Mennonite, we can hardly picture a robust image of evangelism coming out of this separatist group. Much like the fundamentalists who built a fortress mentality to protect doctrine from outside influences, Mennonites withdrew from the "world" to protect their way of life. Shunning the world largely meant having nothing to do with outsiders or the people Christ sent us to "fish" out of the sinful life. But that was not how the Anabaptists felt about evangelism and mission in the sixteenth century. The Anabaptist program of evangelism was actually explosive, spreading to many parts of Europe at that time. Despite opposition and the threat of death, Anabaptists were passionately evangelistic in sharing their faith in Jesus with everyone they met.

Key to the Anabaptist drive to reform the church was the commanding theme of the Great Commission. Jesus said,

> All authority in heaven and on earth has been given to me. Go therefore and make disciples of all nations, baptizing them in the name of the Father and of the Son and of the Holy Spirit, teaching them to observe all that I have commanded you. (Matthew 28:18-20)

In Christ's command, they found the goals of a workable mission strategy and believed it was important to follow the order laid out in these verses. Followers of Jesus Christ must be:

- A people going into all the world
- A people preaching the gospel to every person
- A people prepared for listeners to respond to the gospel presentation
- A people who baptize upon the profession of faith persons who believe in Jesus
- A people who welcome and incorporate new believers into the true Christian church[132]

---

132 Hans Kasdorf in *Anabaptism and Mission* (Scottdale, PA: Herald Press, 1984), 52.

In contrast to the revivalistic program of evangelicalism where "getting saved" is the goal, the Anabaptist program of evangelism involves discipleship.

Luther, Calvin, and other sixteenth-century reformers rediscovered the importance of personal faith in Jesus, but the Radical Reformers rediscovered what they called Nachfolge (discipleship). Saving faith, Anabaptists believed, was just the beginning of our life in Christ. People who heard the message of good news and believed in Jesus as Savior must also recognize Jesus as Lord. To call Jesus "Lord" meant aligning one's life under the life of Christ, submitting all aspects of one's life to the example of Christ, and doing so in accountability to the body of Christ, the church. Living the Christian life in isolation, or as we call it today— "maintaining a private faith"—simply does not fit the pattern of the Great Commission. In short, the disciple of Jesus must be prepared to follow him in every way.

Discipleship was the path to transforming the believer's life and the society in which he or she lived. Christ's teaching and example were the templates for this new life and community. Anabaptists could not conceive of Christianity that made transformation a private and personal affair that had no effect on the external relationships. Where Luther tended to focus on the inner working and experience of grace, Anabaptists saw the focus of the Christian life centering on the outward application of that grace to others. Our relationships with others must be influenced by our discipleship. Harold Bender said that the true test of Christian existence is discipleship.

For the early Anabaptists, obedience to this command was imperative. The Great Commission of Jesus to his disciples in the final words of Matthew was fundamental to individual confession and to the community of believers. They believed it applied to every believer at all times. When arrested and put on trial, their responses were filled with themes of the Great Commission. As one said, "Our faith stands on nothing other than the command of Christ. For Christ didn't say to his disciples: 'Go forth and celebrate the Mass, but go forth and preach the gospel." This was their defense for preaching the gospel.[133]

With the Great Commission playing a central role in the life of discipleship in the individual, the onus to evangelize lay not on the specialists, but on everyone in the community of faith. Whereas the evangelical revivalism relegated the art of converting to dynamic and charismatic speakers, Anabaptists knew that the responsibility for sharing Jesus with others lay with each one of them. This applied to the newest believer as well as the veteran Christian in the church.

Before the Reformation, the ordinary Christian had looked to the religious authorities to lead and guide the church and to "spread" the gospel.

---

[133] Franklin Littell in *Anabaptism and Mission*, 19.

Upon the dawning of the Radical Reformation, the church was no longer in the hands of the wealthy and powerful and educated; now the church was the responsibility of the common man and woman. Franklin Littell offered that, "In Anabaptist opinion, the craftsman might make a better missioner than the cultured man. Jesus himself preached to men in terms of their trade, not with many books."[134] A craftsman who belonged to a guild would have access not only to other craftsmen in his village but in other villages as well. Skilled workers of Anabaptist persuasion who were driven on through persecution to other regions automatically had an "in" with these guilds. Anabaptists were not shy about what they believed, readily sharing the truth of Jesus with whomever they encountered.

Evangelism must be connected to the hermeneutical understanding of Scripture, Anabaptists believed. That meant they took literally the texts of Scripture that charged them to take care of the body as well as the spirit of a person. James challenged his readers to couple faith with action when he wrote,

> If a brother or sister is poorly clothed and lacking in daily food, and one of you says to them, 'Go in peace, be warmed and filled,' without giving them the things needed for the body, what good is that? So also faith by itself, if it does not have works, is dead. (James 2:151-7)

Likewise, the apostle John directly appealed to the centrality of the cross of Christ in caring for others when he wrote,

> By this we know love, that he laid down his life for us, and we ought to lay down our lives for the brothers. But if anyone has the world's goods and sees his brothers in need, yet closes his heart against him, how does God's love abide in him? Little children, let us not love in word or talk but in deed and in truth. (1 John 3:16-18)

It ought to seem absurd to the follower of Christ to preach the gospel to a people whose stomachs are empty. Evangelizing without caring for the physical needs of the people we are witnessing to is inconsistent with the person of Jesus Christ. Anabaptists began to take this seriously and became involved in social justice issues at the beginning of the Reformation and now again in the twentieth century. When we observe the life of Christ, we cannot help but see that he himself "came to set the captives free" and to "preach good news to

---

134 Franklin Littell, *The Anabaptist View of the Church* (Minneapolis, MN: American Society of Church History, 1952), 96.

the poor." We can apply spiritual applications to those metaphors if we want to, but we cannot deny that Jesus demonstrated his compassion for the poor on several occasions— feeding them, healing them, and meeting needs. If we believe this, then we will also subscribe to the revolutionary effect that the inbreaking kingdom of God will have on the world when we choose to follow Jesus in faith and deed.

One of the Anabaptist expressions of mixing evangelism with social justice comes in the form of the Mennonite Central Committee (MCC). They do not pretend to be a missions organization but, as a wing of Anabaptist outreach, envision themselves as complimenting missions efforts around the world. MCC states their goal this way:

> Mennonite Central Committee (MCC) a worldwide ministry of Anabaptist churches, shares God's love and compassion for all in the name of Christ by responding to basic human needs and working for peace and justice. MCC envisions communities worldwide in a right relationship with God, one another and creation.[135]

MCC was originally established to assist Mennonite refugees caught behind the "iron curtain" of Soviet Russia. Over time, it morphed into a relief organization that sought to help all people groups who were in need.

If Anabaptists maintain their original adherence to the Great Commission, their priority will continue to be the gospel proclamation. However, like evangelicals, Anabaptists have become soft in pursuing an evangelistic perspective. Promoting social justice through feeding the poor and caring for the less fortunate is essential to gospel credibility in the world. Yet Anabaptists and MCC initiatives tend to get lost in the physical care aspect and neglect the gospel message. Actions speak loudly to a hurting world, but the world still needs to understand why there is pain and suffering and that it is knowable through biblical teaching.

Combined Strengths

The "revival" approach to evangelism is not working for evangelicalism today. Revival tends to recycle Christians who have known the truth but have fallen away, only to be brought back again. Behind revival methodology is the hope that if the church "wakes up," evangelism will take off and Christians will be emboldened to share the good news with abandon. Not a bad dream, but is

---

135 https://mcccanada.ca/learn/more/strategic-goals

it realistic? Or is it an excuse to sit and wait for a "fresh wind"? Would the church be reinvigorated rather by actually living out the Great Commission?

When people do "get saved," the work has just begun. "Winning souls" for Jesus should not be the pinnacle of evangelism in any sense of ministry. Just as the birth of a child does not signal the culmination but the beginning of life, so too does the salvation of a person only mark "learning to walk" in faith and in the character of Jesus. Evangelical language regarding evangelism needs to move beyond the "decision" as the goal and toward discipleship.

Discipleship, according to the Anabaptist perspective of evangelism, can only be done in community. There are models of one-on-one mentorship in the Bible (Paul and Timothy), but the model Jesus initiated was a community of believers living and working together. Growing in the Christian life was meant to be a lifelong process of mutual accountability and fellowship.

For the Anabaptists, an inclination toward a social gospel tends to distract them from the need to address the sinful nature of humankind. The world wants to see a holistic view of salvation that rescues the sinner and meets her in her present circumstances. When the pendulum swings, however, to the practical side of "meeting needs" without introducing the teaching of Jesus Christ, we are preparing people for judgment on full stomachs. We read frequently in the New Testament that we are to prepare for the Day of the Lord, to be ready, to be awake spiritually, to live holy and God-honoring lives. The message of the cross and the compassionate hand work together to this end.

Evangelical fervor and Anabaptist impulse complement one another and offer a balance to the issue of evangelism. We need the evangelical fervor, that drive to present the gospel to every person, to hear about the crucifixion and resurrection of Jesus Christ, to believe in his name, and to be saved. That passion for mission has been a life-giver to the Anabaptist movement, reminding them of their original calling. Evangelicalism gave rise to the missionary movement and helped to spread the gospel around the world—we cannot forget that. Evangelical passion for the Bible and for preaching Jesus Christ to the masses has inspired Anabaptists to break out of their isolationist tendencies.

We must also remember that evangelicalism was a very socially active movement at one time. Evangelicals worked hard to abolish slavery, to improve the life of the working person, to win civil rights for African Americans and for women. William Wilberforce led the struggle to abolish slavery in British territories due to evangelical influences. Others in America were also active in pursuing the end of slavery on this side of the ocean. That impulse for social justice was not always foreign to the evangelical community.

The Lordship of Christ, that Jesus rules his kingdom now seated at the right hand of God, is a motivating reality for Anabaptists. Kingdom rule and kingdom ethics powerfully influence the meaning of salvation and discipleship. In that spirit, Anabaptists can complement that evangelical fervor with the emphasis of the biblical hope of the kingdom of God breaking into history in tangible ways. The kingdom of God as a political and social reality has not been a natural part of the conversation for some time. Yet the church has been commissioned by the King to introduce the reality of the kingdom through love and service. Evangelicals have a sense of the kingdom coming; Anabaptists preach the kingdom has come. As Anabaptists adopt the fervor of evangelicals for gospel propagation, evangelicals can adopt a kingdom mentality for faith and life from the Anabaptists.

We are often left with the impression from preachers that the task of evangelism is a one-on-one event. Congregants are told they must reach out to their neighbors and single-handedly win them to faith in Christ. That is the impression, anyway. At the beginning of this chapter, I said Jesus implied that "fishing for men" was a team effort, that he sent out his disciples two-by-two to spread the gospel. Contrary to the evangelical, and sometimes Anabaptist, impulse to evangelize as "lone rangers," the Bible often gives the template of a corporate witness as opposed to an individual one. Jesus said that the world will know we are his disciples by our love for one another (John 13:34-35); Paul taught that the testimony of a unified congregation is a corporate witness (Philippians 1:27-28; 2:14-16); and even in our celebration of the Lord's death, we proclaim the death and resurrection of Christ *as a body* (1 Corinthians 11:26). I propose that the witness of Christ does not lay like an albatross on the shoulders of one person reciting the *Four Spiritual Laws* or *Four Steps to Peace* with God but belongs to the corporate effort of the body. Our love for one another, our celebration of Christ, the persecution we face for *being* Christian or choosing a *better way* in the workplace or political arena are as powerful to the watching world as a verbal witness. We do need to be verbal in our witness, but a life of faithfulness and mutual love bears a powerful testimony.

My wife shares a story from her workplace that illustrates a challenge in this regard. A fellow from a branch office of her corporation in a larger metropolis came to her office for a term. He was an aggressive witness for Christ and was "in the face" of many of my wife's co-workers. A co-worker remarked to her, "Those born-agains are sure annoying." My wife replied, "You know I am one of those born-agains too, don't you?" The lady replied that she did know that, but my wife was not "at her" all the time.

Sharing our faith requires a greater finesse than the run-and-gun methods of invasive browbeating. Evangelical styles have been less than respectful to those who have been the object of the evangel. Anabaptists, on the other hand, have been too quiet at times and need to speak up. We need to find the balance of urgency and respect in terms of evangelism.

Evangelism becomes much more than "life-boat" salvation when the two streams work together. When Christians embrace the mission God has given them to reconcile men and women to the Father in heaven, the world we live in transforms. I am not talking about bringing heaven down to earth, creating a utopian experience, but about foreshadowing the culmination of the kingdom that will be when Christ returns. We are showing the world through the way of the cross and community what our world will look like at the *parousia*.

Chapter Eight:
To Change the World – Anabaptists, Evangelicals, and Political Involvement

> (Christ) is the image of the invisible God, the firstborn of all creation. For by him all things were created, in heaven and on earth, visible and invisible, whether thrones or dominions or rulers or authorities—all things were created through him and for him. (Colossians 1:15-17)

People often forget that the Christian faith began in the context of a polytheistic empire that was initially hostile to Christianity. Though Judaism was a legal religion under Roman law, and Christianity was considered an offshoot of Jewish belief, it eventually became clear that followers of The Way were part of an outlaw sect. The Jewish authorities were all too eager to clarify that they had nothing in common with this religion and that Christians did not share their legal status.

If one considers that the Romans declared "Caesar is lord," thereby acknowledging his claim to deity, the Christian declaration that "Jesus is Lord" stands in stark contradistinction. Romans could live with the existence of other gods, but they insisted that Caesar was the only god incarnate. Followers of Jesus, by contrast, could not abide by that insistence since they believed that Jesus alone was God incarnate. Once that conflict was made known, the people of Christ were targets for persecution and execution throughout the empire. Either Caesar is lord or Jesus is Lord; you cannot have both.

For the first three hundred years, the church of Jesus Christ actually thrived under these adverse conditions. Depending on who the emperor was at the time, persecution was either pretty bad or downright terrible. But Christianity spread as the message of the crucified and resurrected carpenter from Nazareth was proclaimed throughout the empire. To be clear, the church of Christ had no affiliation with the Roman government until the fourth century when Emperor Constantine issued the Edict of Milan in 313, legalizing Christianity.

From this period forward, Christianity gained the upper hand as the dominant religion, and all other religions were now persecuted. Statues of Zeus and other gods were defaced, and temples were repurposed or torn down by the suddenly powerful Christian sect. The new church and state relationship blurred the lines of faith and politics, which scholars have termed Constantinianism.

Without going into detail about the erosion of vibrant faith into stale Christendom, Constantinianism weakened the church. Now everyone who wanted to succeed in the empire identified as Christian. It was difficult to tell who the true Christians were from those who merely "went along" with the trends. By the time the Roman Empire fell, Christendom was well-established and the church continued in power based on the template learned from imperial forms. The Reformers looked back on this eleven-hundred-year period as "the apostasy of the church."

A brief summary of this historical snapshot suggests that Christianity and political power do not make compatible bedfellows. When Christians gain dominance in the political sphere of society, the church appears to suffer a lapse in zeal for evangelical faith. Proclamation tends to be supplanted by policy, and the missional church is overcome by peacetime apathy. However, does this mean Christians should avoid political engagement? Given that we in North America do not live under oppressive governments and have the freedom to speak to policy or procedure, do Christians have a moral obligation to take advantage of such freedoms? What does it look like to be politically engaged as Anabaptists and evangelicals or evangelical-Anabaptists?

Before diving into the possibilities, we need to understand the traditional Anabaptist relationship with the ruling authorities and their view of politics. Given their experience of persecution throughout most of the sixteenth century, we can imagine what their views were based upon. Then we can entertain proposals as to how we might change our world without being changed by our world.

Anabaptist Anxieties Concerning the Powers

Like early Christianity, the Anabaptist movement began under hostile conditions. Ulrich Zwingli, under whom Conrad Grebel and his friends studied, had the power and protection of the Swiss Canton of Zurich backing him in his church reforms. The civil authorities worked in harmony with Zwingli to reform the church, but they also restricted him in instituting some of the more radical reforms. This was where the issue of infant baptism came to the fore, and where Grebel and friends pushed for a return to biblical tenets as opposed to civil legislation. When Grebel, Felix Manz, and George Blaurock, together with a small gathering of like-minded believers, broke from Zwingli through being baptized as adults, they were outlawed and forced to run from civil authorities.

Anabaptists were also concerned about the church-state relationship, Constantinianism, arising again and diluting the church as it had done in the fourth century. Zwingli had proven that returning to the New Testament church model was impossible so long as political powers were involved. This experience caused the Anabaptists to foment a long-lasting suspicion of government influence on the church. Unlike the Catholics, Lutherans, and Reformed leaders who enjoyed the political backing of the state wherever they were found, the Anabaptists never garnered that support and, in fact, never desired it. Coincidentally, each of the above-mentioned Christian traditions, together with the civil authorities that backed them, persecuted the Anabaptists in their regions.

There was a deeper, more biblically based concern that prompted Anabaptists to avoid political involvement: their commitment to nonviolence as exemplified by the life of Jesus. Anabaptists knew that law and order were essential to maintaining a civilized existence in any state, but they also knew the government maintained order through the punishing of evildoers and protecting the weak by means of force and coercion. For this reason, they regarded the state as a necessary contribution to society, but an entity devoid of Christ just the same. If the government represented the kingdom of the world, the church represented the kingdom of God. Anabaptists, as a result, developed a radical dualism distinguishing the church from the world that upheld a suspicious view of the state. Their view is summed up by Richard Kyle, "The world is essentially evil and diametrically opposed to the Kingdom of Christ."[136]

For an Anabaptist to be involved in political powers would be an impossibility. They recognized that political participation entailed compromising their faith when voting on or activating the use of force to maintain order. Both the use of force and the use of the oath went against their convictions as per their understanding of the Sermon on the Mount. Even so, given their rejection of political involvement, Anabaptists affirmed that the Christian must obey the state according to Romans 13, where Paul exhorts believers to submit to God-ordained authorities. But when the state invades the spiritual realm, they are out of their jurisdiction. Where the two conflict, the Christian will choose to obey God rather than the state, even at the cost of one's life. This belief led to the long-standing conviction that a "true" Christian cannot hold a government position.

These convictions were first composed as a document known as the Schleitheim Confession of 1527.[137] Under article six "Concerning the Sword," the

---

[136] Richard Kyle, "Anabaptist and Reformed Attitudes Toward Civil Government: A Factor in Political Involvement," Direction Spring 1985 · Vol. 14 No. 1 · pp. 27–33, 29.

[137] The Schleitheim Confession of Faith was a document thought to authored by Michael Sattler of Stauffen, Germany. Originally a Roman Catholic priest, Sattler became an Anabaptist and a leader of the Swiss Brethren who believed in adult baptism. A confession of this nature was a relatively short document of agreed points of faith, which the compilers agreed to keep.

Confession stated that the use of the sword "is outside the perfection of Christ," though it was necessary for putting to death the wicked and protecting the good. Christians were instructed to only use the ban for excommunicating those who sinned—this was the only "force" they were permitted to use. Further on in the article, Christians were not to pass sentence in worldly disputes since Christ did not come to pass judgment between brother and brother in the case of inheritance. Most importantly, because the "sword" was considered an instrument of the state, the Christian had no business being a magistrate (a government official). The Confession states, "Shall one be a magistrate if one should be chosen as such? The answer is as follows: They wished to make Christ king, but He fled and did not view it as the arrangement of His Father. Thus shall we do as He did, and follow Him, and so shall we not walk in darkness."[138] The government magistracy works according to the flesh, and Christians work according to the Spirit. One works in the realm of the world, and the other believes their citizenship is in heaven (Philippians 3:20); the weapons of their conflict are carnal (of the flesh), but the Christians' weapons are spiritual.

You can see how the Anabaptist perspective on the dichotomy of the world and the church would inform their participation in society. Serving in the military was an obvious "no." And since the military or police forces are a necessary instrument of the state, serving as a politician who must protect national interests would mean using force. Even serving as a judge or prosecuting attorney involves casting judgment and handing down a sentence, which an Anabaptist believes is a function of the world. Our task is to reconcile humankind to God, not to condemn. It follows that serving on a jury is incongruous with the Christian mandate to love and forgive, not to judge.

This is the climate that many Mennonites, including myself, were raised to believe in our part of North America. Even five centuries removed, the prevailing ideology is that being elected to a government seat will mean compromising your faith. In the US, it may mean supporting a war; in Canada, it may mean voting for a bill of dubious moral grounding in order to avoid a greater evil. A notable politician of Anabaptist origins was castigated by his home community for voting for an abortion bill which was a clear compromise of Christian conviction. He did this to ensure that women had "safer" abortions and to support his party platform. Therein lies the rub: a Christian may enter politics with the ideal notion of making a difference in the world, but you have to vote the party-way before you can implement changes, if at all. For the Anabaptist wanting to remain faithful to the Sermon on the

---

138 The translation is reprinted from *The Mennonite Quarterly Review*, XIX, 4 (October 1945), 247-253.

Mount and the life of Christ, it is safer to stay out of the political realm altogether than to participate in the world's flawed system of justice.

Being Quiet Does Not Mean "Faithful"

If the radical Reformers created a great commotion in the sixteenth century, they thereafter became a rather benign people in the following centuries. This, of course, is a generalization to make a point since pockets of Anabaptists made an impact on society. But with the intense persecution and death that pursued them through their early years, it is not hard to understand that these simple folks just wanted to live a life of peace and quiet. In fact, they became known as "*die stillen in lande*" (the quiet in the land), a reference to how they kept to themselves and made no overt demands on government policy.

By "no overt demands," I mean they made no demands outside of the privilege of educating their own children in German, military exemption, and other issues pertaining to their own existence. Like the fundamentalists of the early twentieth century, Anabaptists developed a "fortress mentality," an attempt to keep the worldly influences out of their bubbles to remain faithful. They did not want to disrespect the government in any way since they believed that God had ordained those authorities and given them their place, so they kept "quiet" regarding the social policy that affected others.

The Anabaptist perspective on politics was one of withdrawal. This position resembles H. Richard Niebuhr's model of "Christ Against Culture," which takes a negative view toward culture and the state.[139] Since the believing community accepts the Lordship of Christ, they stand apart from the world and its political order. There is no room for compromise in this model, which has resulted in the removal of whole communities to remote parts of the world. Similar but distinct, the separationist model lived in the world and, while separated theologically from the world, struggled for political freedoms. Puritans and Baptists, two examples of this approach, were much more active in political life than the Anabaptists who depended on the benevolence of the government to keep their peace, as it were.

As a people committed to the words of the Sermon on the Mount, withdrawal does not present a consistent testimony. "You are the salt of the earth," Jesus said, and for salt to be useful it must be applied, not hidden in an isolated community (Matthew 5:13). Salt permeates the meat, preserving and flavoring it so that the effect of the application is felt. "You are the light of the world," Jesus goes on to say.

---

139 Richard Kyle, 27.

> A city set on a hill cannot be hidden. Nor do people light a lamp and put it under a basket, but on a stand, and it gives light to all in the house. In the same way, let your light shine before others, so that they may see your good works and give glory to your Father who is in heaven. (Matthew 5:14-16)

For too many long and silent centuries, Anabaptists hid their good qualities from the world so as not to soil themselves with the world. But Jesus commands his disciples in these words to mingle, rub shoulders, and be noticed in society. So the "quiet in the land" schtick does not work when it comes to being faithful witnesses of the goodness of God. Somehow the Anabaptists missed the part where Jesus said, "Don't hide your light," unless they thought the city on a hill was an image to gaze at from a distance. And salt can lose its taste, especially if it just sits there. No, the salt and light permeate and shine through both lifestyle and verbal witness—there is no other way.

Anabaptists have emerged from the shadows in the last century. The Mennonite Brethren have chosen a moderate transformationist position. Their stance on politics is to be selective in how they participate in the political process, but they have recognized the need to be a voice for those who have no voice. Still, how Anabaptists engage the political realm will require some imagination and creativity.

Were They Wrong?

Before discussing the contribution of evangelicalism to the Anabaptist impulse to change the world, to be salt and light, let us briefly consider the Anabaptist understanding of the powers in the world. Were they wrong to vilify so vehemently politics and power as to withdraw from any involvement with civic leadership? Refusing to enter the political realm and accept positions of power and influence as a magistrate or other role, were the Anabaptists exempting themselves from a chance to do some good in society?

Martin Luther believed in a two-kingdom understanding of the world. There was a personal sphere of life and a public sphere of life. His understanding of Jesus' command to "love your enemies" was to relegate it to the personal sphere, to the home, to one's relationships with family and friends, and to the church. In the public sphere, Luther could not see how this command applied to one's civic duty. Ron Sider comments that "Luther went so far as to tell Christians that in their roles as public officials, 'you do not have to ask Christ about your duty.' The emperor supplies the ethic for public life."[140] From the Lutheran perspective, the Christian has a separate duty to the state that exempts him or her from the ethical requirements of the Sermon on the Mount. Luther saw the state as an expression of God's creation, but the church was responsible for the redemption of humankind. They were two different orders requiring separate allegiances. However, reading the text of Scripture we do not see "loopholes" such as the one Luther presented. Jesus made his words applicable to every sphere of life, including the public one. Matters of the court, demands made by the Romans, issues of borrowing and lending, are all issues that Jesus focused on in his teaching. No realm is excluded from the commands to choose Christ-like behavior.

The Reformed position offers a similar application as Luther's regarding Christian involvement in civic affairs. They would say that no responsible Christian can be without concern for civil government. John Calvin did see separate functions for church and state but felt that the state could work for the salvation of humankind. Calvin believed the purpose of Christian involvement in the state was to preserve the freedom of the church. The state was a secondary concern, but an important one that he felt required a working relationship between church and state. That did not mean that the church should be dictated to by the state, for the church held authority over the Christian and Christian life. The state would do its part by providing an orderly context for Christianity to fulfill its mission.

Of the two perspectives, Lutheran and Reformed, North American Christianity predominantly resembles the Reformed position in its relationship to civic responsibility. Evangelical Christianity has clearly engaged the political realm in recent decades with the goal of preserving biblical values and maintaining a context of freedom for the church. Proponents of this ambition have worked hard to use political powers and influences to legislate Judeo-Christian values on American society. Should Anabaptists shift their paradigm on politics and begin to depend on the powers to introduce the kingdom to society?

Since the powers, along with all of humankind and creation, are fallen—that is, corrupted by sin—they are not sufficient for the purposes of ushering in the kingdom of God. In fact, as John Howard Yoder wrote, "We find them seeking to separate us from the love of God."[141] The powers are at work to separate us from the love of God (Romans 8:38-39); the prince of the power of the air rules over the powers that govern those who are far from God's love (Ephesians 2:2); these powers bind us to human rules that have no power to change the heart (Colossians 2:20-23); they, in fact, enslave us to worldly

---

140 Ron Sider, "An Anabaptist Perspective," *Brethren in Christ History and Life*, 28 no 2 Aug 2005, p 255-278, 261.
141 John Howard Yoder, *The Politics of Jesus* (Grand Rapids, MI: Eerdmans, 1994), 141.

principles (Galatians 4:3). Whereas these powers and structures were intended to be our servants, the fall has made us slaves to the powers.

Yoder does not completely dismiss the powers as entirely evil. Yes, they are broken, but we need some form of power structure to maintain order. "Even tyranny (which according to Romans 13:1 is to be counted among the powers) is still better than chaos and we should be subject to it."[142] The law may be used by corrupt officials for personal gain or the manipulation of situations, but the law itself is not evil and should be obeyed. Organization and structure are gifts from God that, though tainted by human sinfulness, continue to express his patience and desire that humankind might seek him as the originator of good (Acts 17: 22-28).

The apostle Paul made three declarations concerning the powers and structures of our world in the Acts text. First, these structures were created by God. Our Lord's purpose for life is that there should be an order that humankind can count on to be the norm. Second, these powers and structures have rebelled and are fallen. Apparently, the powers were not content with the modest purpose they were assigned and desired to possess a higher priority and to rule over humanity. We are mastered then, by their values and made to serve their ends as though they were idols. Indeed, humans worship power and crave control over all things, a complete contrast to the person of Jesus Christ who did not consider equality with God something to be grasped but emptied himself to become a servant (Philippians 2:6-7). Third, even though the powers have rebelled against God, they cannot escape God's purposes, and he still uses them for good.[143]

If the powers and structures of this world are fallen and corrupt, then Anabaptists were not wrong to avoid being part of a corrupt system. To avoid "using" the powers without serving the powers was the mistake. One can use the system without becoming part of an often-unjust system.

What Anabaptists Can Learn from Evangelicals

In the year 2000, Bill and Brad Bright updated a booklet previously published as *Your Five Duties as a Christian Citizen* in 1979. The update added two more duties to the expectations of evangelical Christians so that the new edition is titled *Your Seven Duties as a Christian Citizen*. These duties summed up the political concepts that exemplified the evangelical attitude toward basic involvement in that sphere of life.

---

142 Ibid, 141.
143 Ibid, 142.

The booklet is essentially a call to action by, at the very least, voting in a democratic system. Motivating this call, the Brights employ a scriptural theme, "We have ceased to be the 'salt of the earth' and the 'light of the world,' as Christ has commanded us," and using patriotic lingo to enforce the call, "As a result, the moral fiber of America is rotting away—and our priceless freedom is in grave jeopardy."[144] Setting aside these two motivators for what they are, the Brights have a point to make about basic political involvement. In summary, the seven duties are these:

1. Pray: "Pray that God will send a spiritual awakening to America, that many millions of our citizens will trust in Jesus Christ as Savior and Lord…"[145]
2. Register to vote: "…so you can fulfill your God-given civic duty, fulfilling both your accountability to God and your responsibility to your fellow man."[146]
3. Become informed: This is a call to be informed about the issues concerning government, knowing what the candidates in an election stand for, and to organize and educate others in these matters.[147]
4. Help elect godly people: If it is possible, elect men and women of God to public office at all levels of government and support them faithfully by sharing with them biblical views on the issues.[148]
5. Vote: The challenge here is to vote consistently in every election after informing yourself on the issues. Evaluate the candidates and the issues against the Word of God.[149]
6. After election day, keep going: Voting is not the end, the Brights tell us. Keep working with other godly people "to help bring God back into the public forum…"[150]
7. Make God the issue: This duty has to do with how we see God. Our view of God drives us and determines our actions personally and nationally.[151]

---

144 "Your-7-Duties-as-a-Christian-Citizen-Bill-and-Brad-Bright.Pdf." http://visionamerica.org/wp-content/uploads/2017/10/Your-7-Duties-as-a-Christian-Citizen-Bill-and-Brad-Bright.pdf, p. 5.
145 Ibid, 10.
146 Ibid, 12.
147 Ibid, 14.
148 Ibid, 18.
149 Ibid, 21.
150 Ibid, 25.
151 Ibid, 31.

A closer investigation of these duties will reveal many theological concerns at the foundation of this call, but consider the positives first.

An overarching theme Anabaptists can learn from evangelicals is "ownership." Evangelicals have taken ownership of the nation's issues, committing themselves to being part of the solution rather than armchair critics who do nothing. Christians are citizens of heaven, but we live in the present world system for which we bear responsibility. The separation/withdrawal attitude does not represent the transforming power of the inbreaking kingdom of God to change society. Anabaptists must accept responsibility for the sins of the land and work to bring justice in the midst of broken systems. Evangelicals have taken responsibility in the US for the state of their nation speaking out aggressively on issues contrary to the biblical values they hold dear. That voice may be expressed through becoming informed about socio-political issues, voting for candidates that promote good societal values, and expressing a biblical opinion at "townhall" meetings.

A second theme Anabaptists can learn from evangelicals is to pray for the nation. Though evangelical exegesis in this booklet raises concerns, the biblical basis of this duty to pray bears strong support from the apostle Paul:

> First of all, then, I urge that supplications, prayers, intercessions, and thanksgivings be made for all people, for kings and all who are in high positions, that we may lead a peaceful and quiet life, godly and dignified in every way. (1 Timothy 2:1-2)

Indeed, our prayers ought to include concerns that affect our nations and the leaders who govern *whether we voted for them*. Recently in 2019, Franklin Graham called for prayer for President Trump, a move that inspired some evangelicals while irritating others. The critics' complaint was that Graham was using a prayer event for partisan political purposes.[152] Praying for the nation's leaders is a biblical mandate; praying for leaders as a public display of the church bestowing political support is a dangerous precedent. Pray for your leaders in a nonpartisan spirit—this is good.

Evangelicals have taught us the value of being informed about the social concerns of the nation. They do not have their heads buried in the sand so that they are unaware of the problems of poverty, crime, racial injustice, corporate manipulations, and environmental abuses. Evangelicals tend to be aggressive in

---

152 "Franklin Graham Announces 'Special Day of Prayer' against Enemies of President Trump." https://www.christianpost.com/news/franklin-graham-announces-special-day-of-prayer-against-enemies-of-president-trump.html.

their fight for what they believe is right. Many of their campaigns come across as a "holy war," right versus wrong, and can appear very sanctimonious and judgmental. Without emulating the obnoxious element of being evangelical, Anabaptists can learn from them to be more tenacious in championing the voiceless subjects of injustice. Being informed about what's happening around you while speaking with love and gentleness to the powers demonstrates a Christianity that cares about our world. We want all people to be saved through faith in Jesus Christ, but our care extends beyond the spiritual concerns alone.

Evangelicals are concerned that the right candidates are put in office to rule the region or nation. Not voting indicates a vote for apathy. As in recent elections, one may have to vote for the lesser of two evils, as they say, but to abstain may give power to the greater of the two evils. Anabaptists in the past were concerned that voting for a candidate who advocates a policy they discover to be unbiblical makes them guilty by association. So they did not vote. By not voting, however, they voted not for neutrality but for the winning side, whatever that may be. Today, Anabaptists vote, so the point may seem moot, yet there may be a lingering fear of associating with a candidate who changes his or her position mid-term.

Regardless of past inhibitions, evangelicals who engage politics and social justice issues should inspire Anabaptists in certain respects to emulate their zeal. However, American patriotism more than borders on the idolatrous and shamelessly borrows from Old Testament language to claim status as God's chosen people. They appeal to the founding fathers of the nation as godly characters even though many are proven to be members of the Free Masons. They use Scripture egocentrically, claiming passages like Psalm 33:12, "Blessed is the nation whose God is the LORD..." as proof of God's favor. So there are caveats, a handful of flies in the oatmeal.

The booklet, if it is representative of the evangelical mindset regarding politics, does not represent all evangelicals globally. It presumes that all evangelicals live in free countries, which they do not, and that said political freedom is a gift from God. If an evangelical lives in a closed country, does that mean these principles do not apply? How does one engage in politics in a nation where elections are fixed and despotism reigns?

An Evangelical–Anabaptist Matrix for Political Engagement

We have already discussed how the Anabaptist position on nonviolence makes evangelicals uncomfortable. If Anabaptists reject all use of force and the state faces situations where the police or army needs to mobilize, evangelicals have a hard time seeing how Anabaptists can begin to be involved in political discussion. Can Anabaptists speak into the political process if public order means the use of violence? Can evangelicals envision political and social action that involves alternatives to state involvement in finding solutions?

First, the idea that all political activity involves violence is a fallacy. Most of what a government addresses does not involve the use of violence. Government is more than force; government is necessary for the maintenance of programs and services that promote good health, education, infrastructure, and welfare. So to be involved by speaking to these issues does not compromise the nonviolent conviction held by Anabaptists. Rarely do we see public involvement in a crisis where tactical police units are called out to maintain order; that responsibility belongs to the executives of civil authority.

When it comes to engaging a fallen culture and seeking to reform society, evangelicals must recognize that the agent for transforming society is found not in controlling the Senate or Parliament, but in the church. And Anabaptists must equally recognize the power of the church as God has ordained her to influence society for good. As Sider wrote, Christians are empowered by the Holy Spirit to shape the larger society and express the values of the kingdom through the agency of the church. Only and simply by being the church, living out Christ's calling to his followers to care for the poor, share economically, break down the walls of racial division, maintain marital faithfulness, promote the equality of women, and champion the "least of these" can the church effect change in the world.[153] When society witnesses the community of Christ living out the kingdom ethic of the New Testament, only then can society see that transformation is possible. Since the state is fallen and corrupted by the powers of darkness, Christians ought to recognize that the way to engage political realms is as a prophetic voice from the outside.

That Christians speak a prophetic voice from the outside of government comes from the context of honesty. Sider wrote, "Honesty would demand that an Anabaptist politician tell voters that he or she opposes all use of lethal violence."[154] Indeed, an Anabaptist would not rise very far in North American politics based on that person's nonviolent ethic and commitment to social justice. Even if a Christian who believes in nonviolence does not hold a high office, he or she can still speak to those issues that benefit the common good of society. But to belong to and participate in a system that compromises the tenets of our faith waters down the Christian witness. It becomes very difficult to explain to the observers of the church how and why Christians could compromise their

---

153 Ron Sider, "An Anabaptist Perspective," 258.
154 Ibid, 273.

values for the sake of a policy that hurts the innocent. Being elected to a position need not be the only vehicle through which to effect social change.

Becoming informed about the philosophies and practices of education in our schools is a prime example of what Christians can begin to contribute to society. Since evangelical and Anabaptist students are enrolled in public schools, curriculum involving controversial content becomes the concern of the faith community. It is not just for the sake of Christian students, but all students, all of whom God cares for and desires that they have access to the truths of life. Sex education is but one of those issues that Christian truth can impact and inform.

Anabaptists and evangelicals should and can participate in the discussions that shape the programs and services of civil government to ensure they are fair and ethical. A look at the history of evangelicalism and its campaign to end slavery reveals that the effect of the movement was powerful enough to change the course of British and American politics on the subject. Anabaptists have also been a voice for change through social agencies and peace initiatives.

Above all, the Christian, the evangelical-Anabaptist Christian, a merger of the two streams, will be committed to the Messianic community of Jesus Christ. That citizenship transcends any feelings of patriotism to American or Canadian sensibilities. In working out what it means to be the community of Christ in the present reality, we recognize that being the church is a far weightier calling than maintaining transient political parties that will one day fade away. How many governments have Christians endured in two millennia? And yet, as the monarchies, dictatorships, and democracies come and go, the church remains. Jesus is Lord over those institutions, so the disciples of Jesus speak to them from a place of authority. When governments do not listen to God's people, God acts in history to sustain his church. Where we can be tools of the inbreaking kingdom of Christ, we speak, we act; where we find closed doors, we wait for the Lord to work out his will.

One Example for Social Change

My daughter is passionate about babies and the lives of the unborn. On a recent podcast episode, I invited her to share her thoughts about the banning of abortion in certain US states. She stated that better sex education classes may have a positive influence for change in minority circles.

Often these podcasts are unscripted, so the conversation can go any direction. A question formed in my mind that I felt needed to be asked of a young woman in her twenties. I asked her, "So what do you think the church should do in response to the abortion issue?" I thought I had stumped her.

She paused for a moment and then responded beautifully. The church needs to welcome with arms-wide-open the women who have had abortions and offer them a place to tell their stories. We need to come alongside the suddenly-pregnant without judgment and support them and the life within. It sounds utterly simple, but in truth, the church has not done this well. Congregations have been punitive with the sexually permissive, casting them out of fellowship for violating a core value. However, for the sake of the unborn and the small seed of faith in the mother, congregations need to be overtly redemptive in embracing the young women who "made a mistake." Mistakes can be forgiven.

This may seem simple, but the quiet holocaust has claimed millions of unborn children. One must search the files of one's mind to recall a sermon that encouraged adoption over abortion or welcomed the unwed mother to share her responsibility with the community of faith. Where the underground railroad freed many who were in captivity—and that apart from government sanction—where is the underground railroad for the infant? Should not the evangelical and Anabaptist church be that railroad for change today?

Chapter Nine:
Reading the Bible Together Through the Lens of Trust

We are saved by faith alone. If this is a true evangelical conviction, then all human efforts to improve our world or ourselves as individuals need to be put in context. If we believe that God delivers his children, both in the salvific sense and in the micro-personal sense, we need to practice this faith by trusting in his power, his timing, and his purpose in our situations, and not in human ingenuity or power. It may be that God will use or inspire human ingenuity to solve a crisis, but that is God's prerogative. In any case, to declare *sola fide* (faith alone) as an evangelical needs to be followed up by practical discipleship. In other words, practice what you preach.

What are we preaching? We are preaching that one must put their faith in God. According to John Howard Yoder, "To 'believe' meant, most specifically and concretely in the cultural context of Israel's birth as a nation, to *trust* God for their survival as a people."155 Faith means much more than a cognitive assent to a set of religious principles or how I feel inwardly toward God. Faith means trusting God and acting in such a way that one's ethics line up with the nature of the One in whom trust is placed.

We are saved by faith alone.

Theologically, evangelicals define themselves according to the five Reformation solas:

> Sola scriptura (Scripture alone)
> Sola fide (faith alone)
> Sola gratia (grace alone)
> Sola Christus (Christ alone)
> Soli Deo gloria (glory to God alone)

Sola scriptura defines the hermeneutic of the evangelical, how he or she reads and interprets the Bible. It follows that Scripture stands as the ultimate authority for faith and life. The Bible is not the only place where truth is

---

155 John Howard Yoder, *The Politics of Jesus*, 79. Italics mine.

found, but it is the lens through which one interprets all truths about life. For instance, the Bible is not a science textbook and, therefore, does not tell us everything about the natural world. Theologically, the Bible does tell us that everything we know about the natural world falls under the sovereign power of God.

Sola fide follows by playing a major role in how doctrine is formed. Evangelicals acknowledge that we are saved through faith alone in Jesus Christ and what Christ has done for us through the cross and his resurrection. We are not saved by our own efforts or good works or power or ability; God grants salvation as a free gift despite our sin and the hostility that existed between God and ourselves.

Evangelicals read the Bible on this basis. So do Anabaptists. Both come to the Bible with these solas, although Anabaptists may start with "Christ alone" or a Christocentric understanding of the Bible. Otherwise, they are essentially in agreement.

The difficulty arises from that repetitious Anabaptist refrain of nonviolence. Evangelicals who do not subscribe to nonviolence as a Christian ethic believe that a faithful reading of Scripture based on the five solas does not line up with pacifist conviction. For example, Mark Driscoll, a former evangelical Reformed pastor, once wrote,

> Jesus is not a pansy or a pacifist; he's patient. He has a long wick, but the anger of his wrath is burning. Once the wick is burned up, he is saddling up on a white horse and coming to slaughter his enemies and usher in his kingdom. Blood will flow.[156]

In other words, no pacifist or Christian committed to nonviolence can read Scripture properly without falling over certain texts.

Is this an accurate reading of Scripture? More importantly for this text, can evangelicals and Anabaptists read the Bible with evangelical hermeneutics and a sensitivity to Anabaptist ethical concerns? If we study the Bible with exegetically sound principles, will we find a consistent theme of what it means to put our faith in God? How will the "trust" lens inform our discipleship as evangelicals and Anabaptists?

---

[156] "Is God a Pacifist?" theresurgence.com. http://theresurgence.com/2013/10/22/is-god-a-pacifist.

The Old Testament Testimony

The Old Testament may be a surprising place to begin to unpack a "trust" hermeneutic. If faith in God means trusting him to deliver his people apart from their aggressive participation, what do we do with the war narratives? Most readers of the Bible view the Old Testament as a book of war and violence, where God commands his people to annihilate their enemies. There are truly some gruesome stories with graphic images unsuitable for vegetable-based cartoons.

The contrast of the God of the Old Testament who prescribes violence to advance his kingdom with the God of peace in the New Testament spurred the ancient Christian leader, Marcion, to declare that these were two different gods. He was excommunicated from the church as a heretic. Anabaptists have been accused by some of being Marcionites because they emphasize the New Testament over the Old, even ignoring it altogether in certain contexts and promoting the peace position without explaining the reality of violence.

So what better place to begin than to examine the Old Testament testimony concerning the "trust" lens?

The Exodus Narrative

God's deliverance of the Israelites from Egyptian captivity stands as one of the greatest "escape" stories in the history of the world. Estimates of the number of Israelites leaving Egypt vary, but one can imagine that there were possibly two million people tramping out into the desert. They did not have to dig tunnels like the Allied POWs in the Second World War who attempted to escape in mass from a German stalag; they simply started walking. Of course, the events leading up to this "escape" involved many supernatural occurrences convincing Pharaoh to let the people go.

What makes this narrative particularly astounding is the clear distinction that the Israelites were not participants in the action. They did nothing to bring about the opportunity to leave Egypt; they did nothing to bring about the destruction of the Egyptian army when they were backed up against the Red Sea. Their sole responsibility was to believe and obey what God told them.

> And Moses said to the people, "Fear not, stand firm, and see the salvation of the LORD, which he will work for you today. For the Egyptians whom you see today, you shall never see again. The LORD will fight for you, and you have only to be silent." (Exodus 14:13-14)

One of the earliest lessons for Israel was that God was for them. He would fight their battles if they would put their faith in God. It may be premature to conclude at this point in the narrative that had they been participants in their own deliverance, they may have taken credit for their liberty.

Only three chapters later, we see that Israel took up the sword and fought the Amalekites (Exodus 17:8ff). The reader will note that this does not negate the earlier command to be "silent," since God did not command them to fight. This battle was a result of Moses' frustration with the grumbling of the people, who began to think God was not among them. In this instance, the Israelites fight their own battle…and win! However, the victory would not be possible without the intervention of God in that Moses had to keep his hand up during the fight; if he lowered his hand, the Israelites began to lose. Indeed, many of Israel's victories contain odd tactics and strategies that would not otherwise result in winning the battle. We need only think of the battle of Jericho and the seven-day march that led to the city's downfall as a further example of a peculiar battle technique that gives credit to God.

Taking the Promised Land

If Israel had remained faithful, if their trust had been consistent, the Old Testament narrative would read very differently. God's plan for the taking of the Promised Land originally called for a non-participatory role for Israel for the outcome. Sin, doubting the plan of God, an overall lack of faith, and an inherent desire to do things the worldly way led to a more violent path.

In Exodus 23, the LORD tells Israel that he will send an angel before the people to guard them and to bring them to the Promised Land. The people were to listen to this angel and obey his commands. Rebellion against him would be tragic. Obedience to this angel would, in contrast, result in abundant provision, the absence of miscarriage among the women, plenty of offspring, and a meaningful, fruitful life.

What the LORD says next sounds very different from what actually happened in the conquest of the Promised Land. He says,

> I will send my terror before you and will throw into confusion all the people against whom you shall come, and I will make all your enemies turn their backs to you. And I will send hornets before you, which shall drive out the Hivites, the Canaanites, and the Hittites before you. (Exodus 23:27-28)

A plain reading of the text suggests that the LORD's plan was to slowly scour the Promised Land, driving out the inhabitants by natural means. There is no mention of swordplay or battle plans. Oddly, evangelical commentators do not know what to do with this text. If they employed their hermeneutical skills to the narrative, without question, God's plan for placing his people in the land was nonviolent. Instead, many have tried to find a metaphorical application for the "hornets," rendering them as angels or even some form of battle unit. Yet there is a stark absence of any other metaphor or imagery in the text.

The plain meaning of Exodus 23 obviously continues God's work on behalf of his chosen people. God will do it; they just have to watch. Unfortunately, we are not told why the "hornet" plan did not take effect. One suspects that the rebelliousness of the children of Israel led to a less desirable tactic for conquest. The culmination of rebellion emerges in Exodus 32 when Israel fashioned a golden calf idol while Moses was on Mount Sinai meeting with the LORD. God evaluates the people and tells Moses they are a stiff-necked people, saying he should begin again with Moses as the patriarch of a new people. Clearly, the incident at Mount Sinai revealed that Israel did not trust God to fight on their behalf, instead, questioning his abiding presence. In their minds, they would have to take charge of their own destiny and to do their own fighting. Did God in some fashion acquiesce to their context by allowing them to be involved in the actual conquest? Or did their sinful rebellion disqualify them from God's efficient "hornet" plan?

A Tale of Contrasts

The theme of self-reliance versus trusting God continues throughout the history of Israel. A myriad of examples in the time of the kings of Israel and Judah could be mined to reveal how often the children of Israel failed to trust God. One example of contrast is found in 2 Chronicles with the narratives of King Asa and King Jehoshaphat.

Asa ranks among the godlier kings of Judah in that he did what was good and right in the eyes of the LORD his God, according to the narrator of Chronicles (2 Chronicles 14:2). His reforms included taking away the idolatrous paraphernalia in the land and invoking the people to seek the LORD. And God gave the nation peace as a result. When a large Ethiopian army threatened their national peace, Asa cried out to the LORD for help "against this multitude." Without much detail, the reader is told that "the LORD defeated the Ethiopians before Asa and before Judah." (14:12). Judah's involvement with this battle is unclear, but the victory belonged to the LORD. For many years, the nation enjoyed peace and sought after God by putting away idols and obeying the law.

In the last years of Asa, Baasha, king of Israel, launched invasive maneuvers against Judah. Whereas Asa cried out to the LORD when the Ethiopians invaded, in this instance, Asa relied on political bargaining to solve the dilemma. Emptying the treasuries of the temple, a gross violation in itself, Asa offered the silver and gold to Ben-hadad, a non-Jewish neighbor king, to form an alliance against Baasha (14:3). Hanani the prophet charged Asa with relying on foreign power rather than relying on the God who helped him against the Ethiopians. Hanani reminded Asa, "For the eyes of the LORD run to and fro throughout the whole earth, to give strong support to those whose heart is blameless toward him. You have done foolishly in this, for from now on you will have wars," (14:9). This incident marks a change in Asa in that he ceased relying on the LORD, even when he became ill with a disease.

Contrast this narrative with Jehoshaphat, the son of Asa and the next king of Judah. Again, an alliance of armies came against Judah and all the people gathered before the LORD to seek his deliverance. The Spirit of the LORD came upon Jahaziel, prompting him to speak, saying, "Do not be afraid and do not be dismayed at this great horde, for the battle is not yours but God's... You will not need to fight in this battle. Stand firm, hold your position, and see the salvation of the LORD on your behalf, O Judah and Jerusalem. Do not be afraid and do not be dismayed. Tomorrow go out against them, and the LORD will be with you," (2 Chronicles 20:15 & 17). Jehoshaphat took this to heart and implored the people to trust in God and believe the prophets. He then organized a choir to sing before the army as they went out praising the LORD. We are not given the details of the confrontation except to say that the LORD ambushed the enemy and caused them to destroy each other (20:21-23). Participation of the army of Judah was relegated to observing the LORD act on their behalf.

The flaws of Asa and Jehoshaphat aside, we take away from these incidents the result of what happens when a nation trusts in the LORD. God does the fighting, and the people stand watching the deliverance of the LORD. When the people take military matters into their own hands, they lose badly.

"Woe to Those Who Trust in Chariots"

By the time of Hezekiah, king of Judah, Judah had little left in terms of military resources. When the mighty army of Sennacherib, king of Assyria, laid siege to the known world, he focused on beleaguered Judah, a standout of resistance among the nations. We have seen that Judah/Israel had a long history of syncretism, mixing the worship of Yahweh with pagan deities and making alliances with foreign powers to save them from calamity. Their trust in God wavered from generation to generation. With this next threat, we encounter once again the faithfulness of God in fighting for his people when they call upon him.

The prophet Isaiah spent a considerable portion of his writing warning Judah not to trust in material wealth and the force of arms instead of trusting God. "Woe to those who go down to Egypt for help and rely on horses, who trust in chariots because they are many and in horsemen because they are very strong, but do not look to the Holy One of Israel or consult the LORD," Isaiah wrote (Isaiah 31:1). To the human eye, Egypt appeared to be strong enough to deliver Judah from the clutches of this power-hungry monarch. But from God's perspective, he could see the unobservable weaknesses of the Egyptian army, not to mention the after-effects of trusting a foreign power that does not know when to go home after liberating a land. And Egypt proved to be no match for the Assyrian army.

Hezekiah and Isaiah joined together in prayer, crying out to God as their only hope. Again, the LORD acted in a way that leaves the reader wondering what actually happened. The LORD sent an angel who cut down all the soldiers and officers of the Assyrian army so that Sennacherib was left without an army (2 Chronicles 32:20-23). Sennacherib himself was assassinated by his own sons when he went home. What did the people of Judah do in this battle? Once again, we find that they did not have to lift a finger to rescue themselves from the impending danger. God did it all.

A Prophetic Summary

Even though the Old Testament contains a violent struggle for the national identity of Israel, it does not, in reality, present a justification for violent reactions to earthly threats. Time and time again, when Israel struck out on their own initiative to wrest victory from the enemy, they "struck out." When they had their backs against the wall, they cried out to the LORD and God did things they could not even imagine to deliver them from annihilation.

In answer to the ongoing question of how God will work for his people, Zechariah speaks to Zerubbabel concerning the LORD's modus operandum. Zerubbabel was continuing the work on the temple rebuild and perhaps wondering how the work would be completed. The LORD answers, "Not by might nor by power, but by my Spirit says the LORD of hosts" (Zechariah. 4:6). The connection to all the ways in which the LORD works, including protecting his people, is found in the familiar phrasing of the LORD's eyes roaming over the earth (4:10). This was how Hanani described the omniscience of the LORD to Asa.[157] The same God who sees all things knows all things, and works for his own glory. His power alone will accomplish the task.

We should not, therefore, assume that the violence of the Old Testament accomplished God's purposes for Israel. Human-initiated violence was the unfortunate result of a lack of trust in the power of God to do all he had promised to do for his people. God's own use of violence begs interpretation in these instances, but the issue is human participation in the struggle. One must acknowledge the reality of violence in the Old Testament, and in life in general, acknowledging also that God does command Israel's participation in certain instances of violence. Yet the overall message teaches that God achieves victory for his people without their participation in violence.

The New Testament Revelation

The Gospels continue the theme of the work of God on behalf of his people. God acts in sending his Son, Jesus Christ, into the human situation to achieve a victory of unusual dynamics. Again, the world observes the work of God without assisting in the resulting achievement. Correction: the world participates by violently seizing the Son of God and nailing him to a cross. However, the Triune God orchestrated the crucifixion of Christ, in which the predictable human element unknowingly assisted.

Knowing that humankind would respond violently to the Son of God, Jesus nevertheless was master of the situation. He was in concert with the Father's will in giving himself to death for the sake of human deliverance. He said to the Jews, "For this reason the Father loves me, because I lay down my life that I may take it up again. No one takes it from me, but I lay down my life that I may take it up again" (John 10:17-18). This was the plan.

Victory through Defeat

Human thinking struggles to grasp the concept of losing to win, of accepting defeat to find victory. This strategy confounds the person who loves winning and finds satisfaction only through a resounding whooping of the enemy. That is why the cross creates a stumbling block for so many trying to find meaning in life. Meaning has been defined for so long as "winning"

---

[157] "The eyes of the LORD run to and fro throughout the whole earth..." (2 Chronicles 16:9). Compare with Zechariah 4:10: "These seven are the eyes of the LORD which range through the whole earth..."

that losing simply seems defeatist. Yet the New Testament teaches that Christ achieved victory through suffering and death. In other words, defeat.

To the watching world, a peasant-carpenter from Nazareth with a Messiah-complex was nailed to a piece of wood and died. By faith, the apostles came to understand that this defeat of their beloved teacher achieved a great victory through surrendering to death on the cross. The apostle Paul explained to the Colossians what happened on the cross, saying:

> And you, who were dead in your trespasses and the uncircumcision of your flesh, God made alive together with him, having forgiven all our trespasses, by canceling the record of debt that stood against us with its legal demands. This he set aside, nailing it to the cross. He disarmed the rulers and authorities and put them to open shame, by triumphing over them by the cross. (Colossians 2:13-15)

First, the human spirit was unable to, incapable of, and too weakened to please God through obedience to his law. But God resurrected the human race that was dead because of sin to new life by erasing the debt and its obligations. God did all this—how? By nailing our debt to the cross of Christ. He chose to accomplish this impossible feat through the most unusual means. Historically, nothing of such magnitude had ever impacted this world in such dramatic fashion as the cross of Christ; death achieving life is a paradox. Furthermore, God revealed the folly of human violence by dying as an innocent man on a cross. Paul emphasized that Jesus defeated the powers, shaming them, by being defeated himself.

That Christ's death on the cross stands as an example for those who would follow him finds repetitive emphasis throughout Paul's writing. Earlier in Colossians, Paul wrote, "Therefore, as you have received Christ Jesus the Lord, so walk in him" (2:6). And to the Ephesians, Paul implored the believers to live like Jesus: "Therefore, be imitators of God, as beloved children. And walk in love, as Christ loved us and gave himself up for us, a fragrant offering and sacrifice to God" (Ephesians 5:1-2). These imperatives leave little room for misunderstanding: as Christ submitted to suffering and death for the sake of others, we also are called to come and die with him for the sake of others, literally and figuratively.

To put it succinctly, Christ won the cosmic battle for the human race through a spectacular display of love and sacrifice. All humankind had to do was stand and watch the battle. Our battles will not be won by strength or cunning but by embracing the pattern of our Lord and joining him in submission.

The Lamb That Was Slain

In the book of Revelation, John advances the death of Christ as the source of victory in the cosmic struggle. Reading the Apocalypse, we find multiple ironies related to this victory, John hearing one thing and seeing something completely different, for instance. In 1:10-12, John hears a voice like a trumpet, then turns to see a man. In the throne room scene (5:1-14), John hears that the Lion of Judah is worthy to open the sealed scroll, then turns and sees that the Lion of Judah is a slain lamb (5:6). Again, John hears that the number of the sealed saints is 144,000 (7:4-8), then turns to behold a great multitude that no one can count from every nation and tribe (7:9-10).

John's vision contains a rich depiction of Christological truths, beginning with the loud trumpet-voice. Residing on the lonely island of Patmos, exiled for his confession that Jesus is the Christ, John was not left alone. During his Sunday meditations, John found himself enraptured by the Spirit of God. The voice he heard will have definite connections to the voice Moses heard on Mount Sinai (Exodus 19:16). That voice grabbed his attention as he searched the vision for the source of this authoritative voice, and he turned and saw a figure of a man. Without unpacking all the details of this figure, we will focus on the one relevant to our discussion: John saw Christ portrayed as a kingly and priestly figure. Part of Christ's priestly role was to tend the lampstands as did the Old Testament predecessors. The imagery presents Christ as the caretaker of the churches represented by the seven lampstands. He tends the ecclesial lampstands by commending, correcting, exhorting, and warning the churches so that they may be fit for service as light-bearers in a dark world.

Christ as king and priest reflects the Danielic prophecies of the Son of Man and his identification with humankind while at the same time receiving authority from the Ancient of Days. The Son of Man motif, Jesus' preferred description of himself, plays an important role in the Gospels and here in Revelation, as will be made evident shortly.

Fast-forward to the throne room vision and we read how John was invited up to the heavenly courts to witness a holy sight. After gazing upon the One seated on the throne and the heavenly creatures surrounding him, John observes a scroll it seems no one can open. No one is found worthy to open the scroll and read its contents, which causes great sorrow for John. This is where the Lion of Judah, the Slain Lamb, enters the vision. What makes the Lamb worthy to open the scroll? In his commentary on Revelation, G.K. Beale gives this explanation:

> A human person had to open the book because the promise was made to humanity. But no person was found worthy to open it because all are sinners and stand under the judgment contained in the book (5:3). Nevertheless, Christ was found worthy because he suffered the final judgment as an innocent sacrificial victim on behalf of his people, whom he represented and consequently redeemed (5:9). No doubt he was also considered worthy because he overcame the final judgment imposed on him by redeeming a people and by being raised from death (cf. 5:5-6).[158]

The scroll needed to be opened because it contained the plan of redemption and judgment as prophesied throughout the Old Testament. Opening the seals signifies the activation of that plan for humankind, which believers have longed for over many centuries. That Christ could open it is due primarily to the priestly role we observed in the first chapter of Revelation. Particularly significant for our discussion is the wording used to unveil the One who was worthy to open the scrolls. Jesus is described this way: "Weep no more; behold, the Lion of the tribe of Judah, the root of David, has *conquered*, so that he can open the scroll and its seven seals" (5:5) (italics mine).

Jesus has conquered. Various synonyms are used in other translations, including "overcome" and so on, but the meaning is quite dramatic. Jesus has won a great victory, a seemingly military success. Yet the next verse reveals that the Lion of Judah is also the Lamb that was slain, informing us that the manner of achieving victory was through sacrifice—not just death, but sacrifice.

Now, regarding the 144,000 of Revelation 7, commentators tell us that the numbering John employs bears a resemblance to a military formation. Thus, the twelve-thousands from each tribe are deployed as battalions. Depending on one's interpretation of eschatology, this can mean different things. John hears the number and then turns to see an uncountable number, and one interpretation states that the 144,000 represents the totality of believers throughout history. It is not a literal number. If the number represents the church, in the context of Revelation, "This military force in 7:4-8 conquers its enemy ironically in the same way in which the Lamb has ironically conquered at the cross: by maintaining their faith through suffering, the soldiers overcome the devil."[159] The typical human response to the aggression of self-defense or retaliation finds no place in this Holy Spirit-sealed army of the

---

158 G.K. Beale, *The Book of Revelation* (NIGTC) (Grand Rapids, MI: Eerdmans, 1999), 341.
159 Ibid. 423.

Lord. Rather, following Jesus as the King who conquered our enemy through his suffering and death means imitating his attitude and action.

A Hermeneutic of Trust

Evangelicals love the Bible. Anabaptists love the Bible. Both agree that it is the authority for faith and life in Christian discipleship. If we are careful to use evangelical hermeneutics in reading and interpreting the Bible, I am not sure how we can arrive at any other conclusion than this posture of trust.

To trust in God requires that we abandon typical human responses to crises in our world. Allegiances with ungodly partners or systems to achieve a desired end implies a lack of trust in God's ways and purposes, as seen in the Chronicles narrative. We also have the warnings of the book of Revelation that allegiances with worldly powers will not succeed. The Lord wants us to trust in him even when logic dictates that a compromise would make life easier.

As we have studied in a previous chapter, US evangelicals have all but equated their own specific nation as the new Israel, the chosen people of this dispensation. If that were true, then the US would be called by God to fight like the nation of Israel in the Old Testament—by standing by and observing the unusual maneuvers of God against all enemies that threaten them. However, just as Israel was rebuked by the prophets for trusting in military strength and foreign alliances, the US trusts in its own military industry to protect its values at home and abroad. If these are God's values, they do not need human protection.

A hermeneutic of trust does not apply only to national issues. How each individual approaches the struggles of living in a fallen world with principalities and powers seeking his or her collapse of faith depends on the lens of trust. If we believe God will fight our battles, we will not panic, we will not retaliate, and we will not resort to compromise to ease our discomfort. As Christ suffered in this life, the Bible shows us that as God resurrected him from the dead, so also God can rescue us according to his will.

Chapter Ten:
The Need for Evangelical and Anabaptist Cooperation

Several decades ago, Ron Sider made a comment in relation to the Anabaptist and evangelical question that still resonates today. He said that if evangelicals were consistent, they would be Anabaptists and Anabaptists would be evangelicals. He also said that the two streams need each other as they go forward into the future.[160] I would like to believe this sentiment is still true as we move further into the twenty-first century.

Some, however, have grown disillusioned with the evangelical agenda and would like to see another reformation of the church. US politics revealed a socio-political side of evangelicalism that left a bad taste in many mouths. Evangelicalism has been exposed as particularly "white" and middle class, leaving many non-white and non-prosperous followers of Jesus disenfranchised from the evangelical brand. A plethora of writers have arisen to ask the tough questions regarding evangelicalism with books like *Still Evangelical?* and *The End of Evangelicalism?*

I understand and empathize with the disillusionment, yet I cling to the label with a shred of hope. To me, and I am sure to a great many others, "evangelical" continues to mean "to herald the gospel" or to be a people that proclaim the gospel. My denomination of Mennonites pointedly applied that label to the beginning of our conference name to distinguish us as a gospel-believing and gospel-proclaiming people. We did this to separate our branch of Mennonitism from the legalistic, works-oriented branches of Anabaptism that had lost their way from the grace of Christ.

Perhaps the label has run its course. Does evangelical still mean what it used to mean? Are we at a crossroads where a new name nurtured in the soil of Scripture must arise to define Christians going forward? Or can we wrest the term out of the hands of the hijackers and for once in the history of the church reclaim what rightfully belongs to the people of Christ?

If we are to reclaim the term "evangelical" and marry it to "Anabaptism," we need to understand the purpose of such a marriage. We need to consider

---

160 Norman C. Kraus, 149.

what each stream brings to the mission of representing Jesus Christ to the world and how they can help each other accomplish that mission.

Celebrating What We Have in Common

In many ways, the two branches of Christianity are not that different. A host of shared experiences and values should bind the two together. Misunderstandings of Anabaptism from the very beginning in the sixteenth century have fostered a long-standing cold shoulder to the movement. With the recent resurgence of interest among evangelicals in the last few decades, Christian intellectuals are embracing Anabaptist values as complementary to their own values. Distinct differences remain, but there are commonalities as well.

For starters, we share a common history in the Reformation. Though Martin Luther may be critiqued by the succeeding traditions that emanated from his stand, we are all indebted to Luther for breaking the ice of ecclesial apostasy. His dependency on the state to support church reformation left several of his admirers disillusioned but simultaneously spurred them on to further reforms, including the Anabaptists. Luther's rediscovery of the importance of faith in receiving salvation was monumental for all traditions. Linking faith with a personal encounter with Jesus Christ made Christianity a relational faith rather than a mere institution.

Evangelicals and Anabaptists also share a high view of Scripture as the Word of God. Peter Waldo, the pre-Reformation reformer, was himself transformed by his reading of Scripture, as were John Hus and many others. Luther's own breakthrough came from a study of Romans 1:17 and his consequent research on the grace of God in the New Testament. Anabaptists, with Bibles in their own languages, read and were transformed by their simple, literal reading of the Scriptures. Whenever women and men turned to the reading of the Bible throughout history, revival or renewal has been the standard consequence. Evangelical fervor has always surfed on the powerful wave of biblical literacy, the mere recitation of precious passages convicting the hearts of the listeners. I daresay this shared passion for the Bible needs to continue, nay, be rekindled, as North Americans grow lackadaisical in their attention to the Word of God. We will lose our momentum without a shared dedication to the study of the Bible. We will gain much more if we go beyond reading alone.

Anabaptists were persecuted for refusing to baptize infants and re-baptizing adults who had come to a living faith in the Lord Jesus. In time, however, branches of the faith have accepted the ritual of adult-believer's baptism, including many evangelical traditions. What once was cause for execution has now become commonplace in Protestant circles. How times have changed in that regard. It is unthinkable in our times to imagine that Christians would kill Christians over the symbol of baptism.

With the acceptance of believer's baptism, the principle of voluntary church membership has also become a shared value. During the early decades of the Reformation, one was identified as Roman Catholic, Lutheran, or Reformed (read "Calvinist") based on what region you were born in. Freedom to choose a tradition was unheard of and could be met with familial exclusion and possibly execution if one were to refuse the national religion. As an infant, you would have been baptized against your will into a tradition you would not fully understand until you were older. With voluntary church membership as a guiding truth, people are allowed to choose to believe, choose to belong to a church, and choose to worship God according to what seems biblical to them.

Evangelicals and Anabaptists passionately agree on a deep concern for personal morality, holiness, and a committed Christian walk. Regardless of the distinctives, both can agree that obedience to the commands of Christ is an essential element of vibrant faith.

Shared Struggles

Every church faces the same issues, whether they be evangelical or Anabaptist: How do we keep members from "shopping" other churches? What programs will attract seekers to our fellowship? How intense can we be in applying church discipline to erring members? So even our struggles are shared.

Most evangelical Protestant churches and Anabaptist churches enjoy the freedom of voluntary church membership, but even this shared value comes with difficulties. For instance, while the Anabaptists practiced "adult" believers' baptism in the radical Reformation, the age of baptism candidates continues to slide from high school-aged persons to middle school and even younger. At what age does a young person consciously understand sin and the responsibility of faith? Can ten-year-olds truly devote themselves to a life of discipleship and sacrifice for Christ? All denominations that rest under the free church tradition face this dilemma as parents entrenched in the life of the church anxiously yearn for their children to choose Christ.

Related to the question of baptism is the matter of salvation. Where Anabaptist and some evangelical churches disagree on the doctrine of free will versus predestination, they both continue to wrestle with the origin of salvation. In other words, does the individual initiate salvation when confronted with the gospel of Christ, or is this purely a work of God? It is not simply a matter of Arminian doctrine clashing with Calvinist doctrine; rather, it is a mystery from our earthly perspective concerning who accepts salvation and who rejects this grace. Though we come to the table from different angles, we can agree that the election of believers confounds us all.

Another challenge for both traditions rests in the category of church polity. For North American churches, the democratic model has become a sacred paradigm, as it reflects a cherished form of government. Anabaptists historically operated their fellowships with a congregational approach to decision-making, an ecclesial democracy. Smaller evangelical churches have also found that this model works well for them in a context of mutual trust. However, in the last two decades, churches have grown increasingly fond of what I would call a consumer approach. Family schedules revolve around the athletic pursuits of the children and the artistic activities of dance, music, and high school theater, so that commitment to a membership meeting takes a backseat. People no longer have a desire to sit through reports, squabble over the color of the carpet in the pastor's office, or hear a depressing account of how the membership is failing to meet the budget. They would rather come to church Sunday morning and "enjoy" the worship band and hear a good message. For many, church has become a product.

How do you run a church based on this kind of consumerism rather than as a congregational politic? Congregational polity, for all its flaws, offers an egalitarian dynamic whereby every member has a say in the life of the church. All opinions are of equal weight. But are all congregants equal in their understanding of theology or doctrine? Are all congregants equal in their grasp of business and governance? How often do we secretly find ourselves annoyed with that member who carries a ton of influence but has no idea what they are talking about? Congregational government has failed the members enough that membership meetings are to be avoided.

Enter the CEO-style polity that offers a streamlined form of leadership that puts the responsibility of decision-making in the hands of the few or the one. We see this paradigm acted out in the mega-church for the most part, but smaller churches have taken note and are envious of their larger counterparts. Even the small congregation wants this polity as long as the pastor carries a truckload of charisma. Another name for this polity is the personality-driven church; the pastor is the star, the face of this organization. Success rises and falls with the character and dynamic nature of the pastor as he or she leads the church from the top-down. Congregants are content to leave the decisions to these gifted personalities so long as they stay pure, blameless, and accountable. Is there accountability in this model?

Popular culture has witnessed that no one in the spotlight is safe from the scrutiny of the masses. Social media informs us of the goings-on of celebrities and their failings. From Tiger Woods' private life to the backroom immorality of Harvey Weinstein, high-profile individuals have fallen from grace. That includes pastors and well-known Christian leaders. With a scandal-ridden celebrity, one may stop watching their movies or listening to their music. But when a scandal rocks the personality-driven church, when a pastor falls, the spiritual consequences cannot be measured in dollars and cents like a fallen pop star. People leave the church and possibly the faith because too much power was placed on a personality rather than on Jesus Christ.

Anabaptist and evangelical branches of the faith face these twenty-first-century problems together. None of us are immune to the age-old sinful attitude expressed by the Israelites, "Give us a king like the other nations." In an age of blurred lines of doctrine and practice, a desire to find common ground and ecumenical unity, what do the two branches have to offer each other in mutual cooperation?

Why We Need Each Other

"Anabaptist" has become a moniker for those who embrace the Anabaptist vision even though they are not traditionally or culturally Anabaptist. "Mennonite" has been dropped from many church signs because of the cultural identification it portrays. We do not want people to think they have to be Mennonite to come to our churches. We do not want them to think they have to speak a dialect of German or eat certain foods to fit into the social and spiritual life of our fellowship. Consequently, Mennonite churches have become nameless or quietly Anabaptist as their signs indicate merely that they are a fellowship, chapel, or tabernacle, while the Hauerwases, McKnights, Fitches, and Stuarts boldly carry the distinction of being Anabaptist.161 Mennonites have even left Mennonite churches to join non-denominational churches, while others catch the Anabaptist vision and take their place. It's quite bizarre to observe the seating change.

Evangelicalism has had a role to place in this musical-chairs game. When confronted with evangelical values, Anabaptists have been challenged to consider their cultural blind spots. The call to mission, for instance, has been influential in confronting Mennonite leadership with its use of language and cultural terms to be more inclusive of those entering the fellowship from other cultures. Rather than cling to the homogenous nature of our congregations, we were challenged by the evangelical value of Christ-for-all-peoples to

---

161 These are surnames of well-known authors and professors who, coming from non-traditional Anabaptist origins, have embraced Anabaptist principles as being in keeping with biblical truths.

become multicultural. An ongoing process of sorting theological convictions from ethnic conventions has benefited the Anabaptist churches in becoming more missional. The faces of the congregations in urban settings are no longer merely white but include Latino and Asian and African.

Conversely, while evangelicalism has helped Anabaptists to widen the invitation of our churches, Anabaptists have helped evangelicals to think seriously about making disciples. Evangelical churches have adopted a "Walmart" mentality of building big structures to seat large numbers of worshipers seeking a concert-like experience with polished messages. The "bigger-is-better" model of American society has continued to influence church culture so that, like Walmart, mega-churches appear to offer what the small church cannot—programs, professionalism in worship, and corporate organization that handles political workings so that you don't have to. Even the small churches put pressure on their pastors to emulate the big churches.

In the largess of it all, the personal and relational aspects of being the body of Christ may get missed. Accountability—recognizing when someone did not make it to worship today—gets lost in the crowd. More than that, personal involvement through the study of the Word of God and walking with each other in the pain of life, may not happen in the big church. Yes, small group options exist, but not everyone feels comfortable in those settings. Anabaptists have typically gravitated to small fellowships for the purpose of being a family. Evangelicals could learn from that and rethink the big-box-store methodology of doing church. Instead of salting our urban centers with churches in every corner, we have begun clumping together like a salt lick in one corner of the city. How are we spreading the salt and light by huddling in one place?

Another related connection for Anabaptists and evangelicals is our mutual need to represent the kingdom of God. In other words, both traditions need to confess that we do not have all the answers to the questions of faith and life. It is altogether too easy to stray from our common affirmation that the center of our faith is a personal living relationship with Jesus Christ. For evangelicals, the tendency may be to individualize faith to the extent that the community of faith is an option rather than a necessity to spiritual growth.[162] Anabaptists need to remind evangelicals that being in relationship with Christ means relating to his body, the gathered church. Jesus said that he is the head of the body and we are the members of that body. It is therefore

---

162 In light of the discussion of the draw of big-box churches, this is an odd development. The larger the churches we build, the more individualistic faith seems to grow. Though we gather in enormous worship buildings, we are cut off from accountability or ownership of the body. We can come and go as we please.

impossible to call oneself a Christian and not be connected to other believers in a mutual relationship of caring and giving and serving together.

That personal living relationship with Jesus Christ must be guarded, as the apostle Paul said, from substitutes that threaten to take his place. Evangelical values remind Anabaptists that ethnic distinctions cannot replace gospel truth. Even doctrinal positions can subtly threaten the central place of Christ in the Anabaptist perspective, such as when the peace position takes a dominant position. Some Mennonites have declared that "peace is the heart of the gospel," suggesting that peace was the sole reason Jesus came to dwell with humankind. Others would retort that the heart of the gospel rests in the love of God for humankind and that peace is the fruit of that loving act on the cross. Evangelical truth has helped balance that tension and remind Anabaptists that "peace at all costs" does not necessarily represent Christ, who came to bring division even between family members for the sake of the gospel.[163] Peace alone can become an idol that detracts from the person of Christ and confuses the person seeking a relationship with him.

Concern for a balanced evangelistic approach needs to be a priority for both perspectives. Evangelicals have consistently stressed the need to spread the good news of Jesus to those who have never heard. On the other hand, Anabaptists have developed their strategy for evangelism with a humanitarian emphasis. They have been accused of being promoters of a social gospel that focuses too much on empty stomachs. In the past, Anabaptists may have rested in the idea that living the gospel is a witness that needs no verbalization. Evangelicals, however, need to be more holistic in their witness; they have often neglected to inform the seeker that costly discipleship comes with believing in Jesus. The one focuses on the spiritual transformation at the expense of physical needs, while the other needs to be more rigorous in witnessing for the risen Christ.

As the pendulum swings back and forth, we can see that neither perspective of Christianity has superior leverage. We are like the proverbial puzzle—one piece filling in the vacancy left by the other and vice versa.

---

[163] "Do not think that I have come to bring peace to the earth. I have not come to bring peace, but a sword. For I have come to set a man against his father, and a daughter against her mother, and a daughter-in-law against her mother-in-law. And a person's enemies will be those of his own household. Whoever love father or mother more than me is not worthy of me, and whoever loves son or daughter more than me is not worthy of me. And whoever finds his life will lose it, and whoever loses his life for my sake will find it." (Matthew 10:34-39)

Epilogue:
Merging but Not Emergent

As a child, I looked forward to family vacations when we would go camping or take a trip. Traveling to the US was always exciting because it was like going to a different country, which of course, it was. But I look back with humor on those vacations when we could see our parents in a different context and find out who they really were inside.

I remember on one trip to the US when traveling on the big highways and navigating from one trunk of road to another. It was especially memorable for me when we were back in Canada when my mother exclaimed, "Canadians don't know how to merge." I suppose she observed the flow of traffic down south and how seamless it must have been compared to our own urban experience. It was true in our context—when Prairie Canadians came to a "yield" sign, they did not try to merge; they stopped altogether. Those signs may as well have been painted red and been cut eight-sided. That manner of "merging" brings the flow behind you to a complete standstill.

I wonder if Anabaptists and evangelicals know how to merge.

The two branches of Christian faith need to merge but not become emergent. The emergent church has given way to Progressive Christianity, a new path that takes the Bible less seriously and is quite tolerant of, well, everything.

The emerging church was a Christian movement of the late twentieth and early twenty-first centuries. Members of almost all Christian traditions contain groups that would identify as emergent. What are they emerging from, you may ask? Disillusioned with the labels of "conservative" and "liberal," emergent Christians seek to remove distinctives and unify them into one voice. They are emerging, if you will, from the divisiveness of the Christian church to become "one" with all who call themselves Christians. That does not sound terrible until you consider that the distinctives they seek to remove may be the core values of your tradition.

Their emphasis is dialogue. Again, dialogue is good. We need to hear each other, to consider what the person across the table believes is important. However, if dialogue leads to the deconstruction of fundamental truths for the sake of harmony, we are left with a vanilla faith—no toppings, which is kind of boring.

I am not opening a new discussion here on the emergent church. I am saying bringing evangelicals and Anabaptists together does not mean scrapping core values for the sake of unity. Rather, merging the two streams—the two branches of the tree of Reformation—means taking the best of both and complementing each other.

All my life, I believed I was living as an evangelical-Anabaptist. In the last few years as I have studied, prayed, and meditated on this more and more, I realize I have much to learn about this "merging." And yet it is profoundly simple.

> I am an evangelical-Anabaptist.
>
> I love Jesus Christ, the Son of God.
>
> I am baptized as an adult who chose to believe in Jesus.
> I follow him and strive to be like him as a disciple follows his or her master.
>
> I believe following Jesus means responding to a violent and hostile world in a nonviolent way. I believe that I am called to the way of love, not the way of force.
>
> I study the Bible to know him better. I believe that the Old and New Testaments have something to say to us about who God is and how his mission was accomplished through his Son, Jesus Christ.
>
> I am committed to engaging and supporting missional efforts to make the name of Jesus known in the world. I believe in the propagation of the gospel for the salvation of those whom God would call.
>
> I am a witness to the resurrected Christ.
>
> I anticipate the return of Jesus Christ whenever that may come, and in whatever fashion he chooses to come, and will live as one prepared for that event.
>
> I am an evangelical-Anabaptist.

Bibliography

Aulen, Gustaf. *Christus Victor: An Historical Study of the Three Main Types of the Idea of the Atonement.* Eugene, OR: Wipf and Stock, 2003 (translation).

Beale, G.K. *The Book of Revelation.* Grand Rapids, MI: Eerdmans, 1999.

Bender, Harold S. "The Anabaptist Vision." *Church History 13.1*, 1944: 3-24.

Bonhoeffer, Dietrich. *The Cost of Discipleship.* New York: Macmillan Publishing House, 1963.

Bright, Bill. *Your 7 Duties as a Christian Citizen.* October 2017 (accessed May 30, 2019).

Burkholder, Jared S. *The Activist Impulse.* Eugene, OR: Pickwick Publications, 2012.

Clapp, Rodney. *A Peculiar People.* Downers Grove, IL: InterVarsity Press, 1996.

Darby, John Nelson. *Lectures on the second coming.* London: G. Morrish, 1909.

Dyck, Cornelius J. ed. *An Introduction to Mennonite History: A Popular History of the Anabaptists and the Mennonites 3rd ed.* Scottdale, PA: Herald Press, 1993.

eds., Jared S. Burkholder and David C. Cramer. *The Activist Impulse: Essays on the Intersection of Evangelicalism and Anabaptism.* Eugene, OR: Pickwick Publications, 2012.

eds., Joanna Harader and A.O. Green. *A Living Alternative.* New York: Ettelloc Publishing, 2014.

Erickson, Matt. "The Disturbing Temptations of Pastoring in Obscurity." *Christianity Today*, March 14, 2019.

Fitch, David. *The End of Evangelicalism.* Eugene, OR: Cascade Books, 2011.

France, R.T. *The Gospel of Mark.* Grand Rapids, MI: Eerdman's Publishing Company, 2002.

Groothuis, Douglas. "The Postmodernist Challenge to Theology." *Themelios* 25, no. 1 (November 1999): 4-22.

Henderson, Charles. *Godweb.* n.d. https://www.godweb.org/leftbehind.htm (accessed April 12, 2019).

Hiebert, Frances F. "The Atonement in Anabaptist Theology." *Direction: A Mennonite Brethren Forum* 30, no. 2 (2001): 122-38.

Hiemstra, Rick, and Stiller Karen. *In Trust Center for Theological Schools.* 2016. https://www.intrust.org/Magazine/Issues/New-Year-2016/Religious-affiliation-and-attendance-in-Canada (accessed March 12, 2019).

Johns, Loren L. "Conceiving Violence: The Apocalypse of John and the Left Behind Series." *Direction: A Mennonite Brethren Forum* 34, no. 2 (2005): 194-214.

Keller, Timothy. *King's Cross.* New York: Dutton, 2011.

Kraus, C. Norman, ed. *Evangelicalism and Anabaptism.* Scottdale, PA: Herald Press, 1979.

Kyle, Richard. "Anabaptist and Reformed Attitudes Toward Civil Government: A Factor in Political Involvement." *Direction: A Mennonite Brethren Forum* 14, no. 1 (1985): 27-33.

Labberton, Mark, ed. *Still Evangelical?* Downers Grove, IL: InterVarsity Press, 2018.

Lederach, Paul M. *A Third Way.* Scottdale, PA: Herald Press, 1980.

Lindsey, Hal. *The Late Great Planet Earth.* Grand Rapids, MI: Zondervan, 1970.

—. *The Rapture: Truth or Consequences.* New York: Bantam, 1983.

Littel, Franklin H. *The Anabaptist View of the Church.* Minneapolis, MN: The American Society of Church History, n.d.

Longenecker, Richard. "Major Tasks of an Evangelical Hermeneutic." n.d.

Longman III, Tremper. *Daniel: The NIV Application Commentary.* Grand Rapids: Zondervan, 1999.

Middleton, J. Richard. *A New Heaven and a New Earth.* Grand Rapids, MI: Baker, 2014.

Murray, Stewart. *The Naked Anabaptist: The Bare Essentials of a Radical Faith.* Scottdale, PA: Herald Press, 2010.

Noll, Mark. *The Rise of Evangelicalism.* Downers Grove, IL: InterVarsity Press, 2003.

Nolt, Harry Loewen and Steve. *Through Fire and Water: An Overview of Mennonite History.* Scottdale, PA: Herald Press, 1996.

Plett, Delbert. *Saints and Sinners: The Kleine Gemeinde in Imperial Russia 1812 to 1875.* Steinbach, MB: Crossway Publications, 1999.

Plett, Harvey. *Seeking to be Faithful.* Steinbach, MB: Evangelical Mennonite Conference, 1996.

Reimer, James. *Mennonites and Classical Theology.* Kitchener, ON: Pandora Press, 2001.

Roth, John. *Beliefs: Mennonite Faith and Practice.* Scottdale, PA: Herald Press, 2005.

Shenk, Wilbert R. ed. *Anabaptism and Mission.* Scottdale, PA: Herald Press, 1984.

Sider, Ron. "An Anabaptist Perspective." *Brethren in Christ History and Life* 28, no. 2 (August 2005): 255-278.

Simons, Menno. *The Complete Writings of Menno Simons.* Scottdale, PA: Herald Press, 1984.

Smith, Wilbur M. "The Prophetic Literature of Colonial America." *Bibliotheca Sacra*, March 1943: 67-82.

Storms, Sam. "10 Things You Should Know About the Satisfaction Theory of the Atonement." *http://www.samstorms.com*. April 3, 2019. http://www.samstorms.com (accessed May 10, 2019).

—. *Kingdom Come*. Ross-Shire, Scotland: Mentor, 2013.

Stott, John R. W. *The Message of the Sermon on the Mount*. Downers Grove, IL: InterVarsity Press, 1978.

Svigel, Michael J. "What Child is This?: Darby's Early Exegetical Argument for the Pretribulation Rapture of the Church." *Trinity Journal* 35, no. 2 (2014): 225-51.

Wacker, Grant. *Teacher Serve from the National Humanities Center*. October 2000. http://nationalhumanitiescenter.org/tserve/twenty/tkeyinfo/liberal.htm (accessed 2019).

Wilkinson, Alissa. *The "Left Behind" Series Was Just the Latest Way America Prepared for the Rapture*. July 13, 2016. https://www.washingtonpost.com/news/act-four/wp/2016/07/13/the-left-behind-series-was-just-the-latest-way-america-prepared-for-the-rapture/ (accessed April 3, 2019).

Yoder, John Howard. *The Politics of Jesus*. Grand Rapids, MI: Eerdman's, 1994.